Europe's most wanted man:
the quest for
RADOVAN KARADŽIĆ

Nick Hawton was the BBC's Foreign Correspondent in the former Yugoslavia between 2002–08. He has written extensively on war crimes issues, including the case of Radovan Karadžić, for the BBC and for *The Times*. He graduated in Modern History from Oxford University and currently lives in Sarajevo with his wife and young daughter.

Europe's most wanted man:

the quest for RADOVAN KARADŽIĆ

Nick Hawton

arrow books

Published by Arrow 2010

2 4 6 8 10 9 7 5 3 1

First published in Great Britain in 2009 by
Hutchinson
Random House, 20 Vauxhall Bridge Road,
London SW1V 2SA

www.rbooks.co.uk

Addresses for companies within The Random House Group Limited can be found at:
www.randomhouse.co.uk/offices.htm

The Random House Group Limited Reg. No. 954009

A CIP catalogue record for this book
is available from the British Library

ISBN 9780099525431

The Random House Group Limited supports The Forest Stewardship
Council (FSC), the leading international forest certification organisation. All our
titles that are printed on Greenpeace approved FSC certified paper carry the FSC logo.
Our paper procurement policy can be found at www.rbooks.co.uk/environment

Typeset by Palimpsest Book Production Limited,
Grangemouth, Stirlingshire

Printed and bound in Great Britain by
CPI Bookmarque, Croydon CR0 4TD

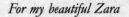
For my beautiful Zara

Contents

Acknowledgements

There are many people whom I would like to thank for making this book possible.

At the BBC, I would like to thank Peter Burdin, Mark Brayne and Malcolm Downing for giving me the opportunity and the privilege to work for the BBC in the Balkans, and David Ross and David Lewis for believing that this story needed to be investigated.

I would like to thank the excellent BBC Correspondents and good friends, Allan Little and Malcolm Brabant, for their pithy words of wisdom and their solid advice about how on earth a rooky foreign correspondent should deal with the incredibly complicated and fraught-with-risk former Yugoslavia.

At *The Times* newspaper, I would like to thank Martin Fletcher and Richard Beeston who truly believed in the value of foreign news and who fought to keep it on the front pages.

I thank my agent Sonia Land for believing in this project from the start and for her enthusiasm and determination to turn it into reality. I also thank Lucy Fawcett and Gaia Banks for their support and hard work. I would like to thank my editors at Random House and Hutchinson, Paul Sidey and James Nightingale, for keeping me on the straight and narrow and making me see the wood for the trees.

There are my fellow journalists who travelled along many of the same roads as myself and who reported on Bosnia when everyone else had gone home: Daniel Skoglund, Markus Bickel, Beth Kampschror and Erich Rathfelder and, later on, Thomas Roser and Neil McDonald. Your ideas and wit kept me going.

Thank you to Ivana and Iva and Patrick, Isabeau, Javier,

Stephen and Charles for listening to my ramblings and theories and testing everything I said. Igor, thank you for your car and your well-placed cynicism. Adrian Wilkinson, thank you for everything.

There are some people whom I cannot mention by name. As the saying goes, you know who you are. Thank you for trusting me and telling me what you did. You enabled me to see the full picture.

This book was a long time in the making. My friends and relatives put up with good grace my never-ending chatter about the subject. Thank you all, especially my mother and my cousin Mark for his home and his humour in The Hague. My wife gave me her suppport, patience and commonsense advice beyond the call of duty.

This book would not have happened without the encouragement, the skill and the words of my father.

There are two people who opened my eyes and made everything possible: Milorad Batinic (Lola) and Alisa. You know what you did. I am for ever grateful for your time, your wisdom and your generosity.

I would also like to thank all the people who appear in this book. I listened to what you had to say and I thank you for telling me your stories.

This is not a book about judgement. It is a book about what I found.

Europe's most wanted man:

the quest for
RADOVAN KARADŽIĆ

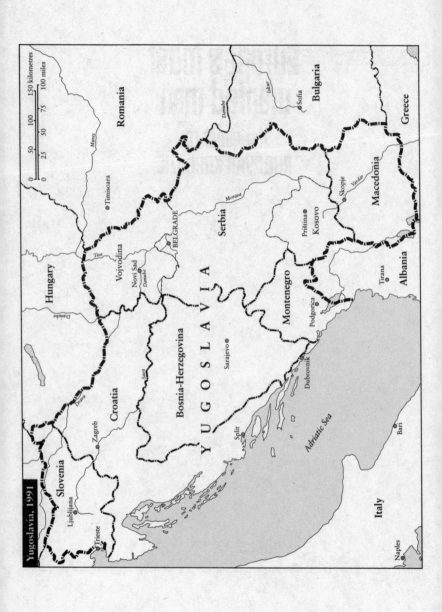

Yugoslavia, 1991

Post-Dayton Bosnia-Herzegovina, 2009

CROATIA

REPUBLIKA SRPSKA

Banja Luka

BOSNIA-
HERZEGOVINA

SERBIA

Zvornik

Srebrenica

CROATIA

Sarajevo   Pale

FEDERATION OF
BOSNIA-HERZEGOVINA

Split

Mostar

REPUBLIKA
SRPSKA

Šavnik

MONTENEGRO

Nikšić

Dubrovnik

Adriatic Sea

Podgorica

| 0 | | | 50 | | 100 kilometres |
| 0 | 10 | 20 | 30 | 40 | 50 miles |

Prologue

The doors to the number 73 bus shuddered to a close and he settled himself down in a seat near the front. An old lady kindly offered to stamp his ticket in the machine. He was laden with bags: the white plastic one with the newspapers and CDs, the haversack with his laptop and the raffia bag with his other stuff. But it was not a long journey and he would be there soon. He was behind schedule, but there was no need to worry. They would not mind. He glanced out of the window, turned back, pulled out some reading glasses and opened his religious book.

The bus moved off, continuing its journey through the urban sprawl on the outskirts of the city. It was the end of the week and the main rush hour was over. There were only around a dozen or so people on board. Eventually, the tower blocks slipped away and the horizon opened out into the familiar low-rise buildings of Zemun. In the past, this area had been a town in its own right, situated on the banks of the Danube, but these days it was just another suburb of the Serbian capital. It was mid-summer and still quite warm, even at this hour. In the distance, he could see the first hints of darkness creeping out of the eastern sky.

He was going away for a few days' relaxation. He had felt under pressure for some time. There had been moments in the past when he had felt jumpy, but this time it was different. He felt the net might be closing. He remembered the time a police van had stopped in front of him and a group of officers had jumped out. They had run towards him and, just as he thought they were about to seize him, continued past in pursuit of some other wanted man. He had smiled to himself at the time, though the fear had been real enough. But these days he sensed that things were different, that maybe they finally were getting close. If he could just last until the end of the year things might still work out. He glanced around the bus from under the brim of his hat. He caught the eye of the old lady who was standing behind him. She was trying to read his book. Even now he could not be sure that he was not being followed.

The bus pulled up and the doors all creaked open. He was conscious that more people were getting on but he kept his head down and continued to read. The doors closed and the old bus jerked back on to the road. He pulled his bags closer. His fingers traced the edge of the laptop through the haversack's material as if to reassure himself it was still there. He would use these next few days to do some more writing, away from the hustle and bustle of the big city and the pressures of dealing with his patients. He had told friends he was going to Croatia for a few days.

He pulled the hat lower over his eyes, sensing that someone was staring at him from behind. Or was it just his imagination? He felt tired. The bus stopped again and this time he glanced up towards the front and saw two policemen get on. They stood next to the driver. The doors closed and the bus pulled away. He sighed and turned to gaze at the fields, green and summer yellow, which stretched into the distance. This was not his real home, these were not the mountains of Bosnia or Montenegro. But over the years he had built a new life here. At least these were his people and he certainly felt safer here. This was now home. He noticed the two policemen were now talking to the driver. The bus was slowing. Suddenly he was aware of two more policeman approaching him from behind.

They pushed passed the old lady, showing an ID card. One of them leaned over and spoke: 'Don't move. We know who you are. We've been following you for some time.'

Immediately, they leaned forward and each grabbed one of his arms. He felt his hat and glasses slip from his head. As they pulled him to his feet he grabbed for his rucksack and raffia bag. But he could not reach his plastic bag. The policeman picked it up instead. He looked at the woman standing in front of him. She looked shocked and was remonstrating with one of the officers, asking why they were doing this to an old man. He could see in the eyes of his two captors that there was no point in arguing. This *was* the moment. He did not resist.

Glancing around at the other passengers, he became aware of the other policemen on the bus. There must have been three or four in uniform and at least one other in plainclothes. He was being ushered towards the front door. There was no escape, no point in even thinking about it. He had hoped it would never come to this. Just a few more months and he would have handed himself in to the authorities anyway. Just a few more months.

One of his captors shouted to the driver to stop. The bus pulled over and the front door opened. He reached the steps and began to descend. What of his friends now? What about his patients? What about his family in Bosnia? He was half pulled, half pushed down the stairs. He almost lost his footing and stumbled forward, reading glasses slipping down his nose and hat falling over his eyes.

As he reached the tarmac, he felt the pressure releasing, a new reality dawning in his mind. For a moment he was lost, not knowing in which direction to walk. The bus had pulled up in between stops. Up ahead was the old disused police checkpoint, a blue hut next to the road, these days covered in torn posters and graffiti. Behind was Zemun and the main road into Belgrade. His legs felt weak. A hand gripped his elbow and propelled him around. There was a car ahead and they were walking him towards it. He heard the engine of the bus start to rev and he turned to look back. He could see some of the passengers standing up; some were staring out of the window, others seemed to be arguing with the driver. But the bus was already moving off down the road.

They reached the car and the man holding his elbow used his spare hand to open the door. They pushed him inside. There had not been a word spoken since they had left the bus. Another man got in next to him, guards to either side, their bodies pressing against his. The car doors slammed and the tyres screeched on the gravel of the lay-by before they sped back towards Belgrade, retracing the route of the number 73 bus.

Another feeling came over him then: suddenly he felt free. The running, the hiding, was finally over. A new reality was beginning. Even now he was aware that things would never be the same for him again; that the shadow life he had created and lived for so long was dissolving.

The rows of tower blocks signalled that they were entering Belgrade. There were still some late-evening commuters waiting at bus stops for the trip home. The car crossed the bridge over the river. They were not far from the Red Star Belgrade football stadium. Red Star was the team he had always supported. He was now certain where they were headed. They passed the military hospital and then the car slowed. One of the men next to him rummaged in his pocket and pulled out a blindfold.

'We have to do this.'

He knew the procedures. The man put the blindfold over his head and pulled it down over his eyes. The world went black. For a minute he felt disorientated. He knew that when the blindfold was lifted off his life as Dragan David Dabić would be over. He would once again be his true self.

It was 9.45 p.m. on Friday 18 July 2008. After more than ten years on the run, Dr Radovan Karadžić, former Bosnian Serb President, former psychiatrist, one-time poet and war crimes fugitive, was in custody. Prosecutors at the International

Criminal Tribunal for the former Yugoslavia (ICTY) had charged him *in absentia* with genocide, complicity in genocide, extermination, murder, wilful killing, persecutions, deportation, inhumane acts, unlawfully inflicting terror upon civilians, and the taking of hostages. He was accused of helping to mastermind one of the most brutal and murderous regimes in modern European history.

He had managed to evade countless arrest operations and had seemed impervious to the attempts made by NATO peacekeepers, by numerous intelligence agencies and individual bounty hunters, to track him down. Even a $5 million reward had failed to produce results. His mystique had increased to such an extent over the years that, by the time he was arrested, he had become a near-legendary figure to his supporters.

And he had not been idle during his time on the run, pursuing his career as a writer and poet, even having some of his works published. Most recently, he had set himself up as an alternative healer, appearing at public seminars and creating his own website. He had a regular circle of friends and had been living a relatively normal and comfortable life in an apartment on the outskirts of the Serbian capital.

But how had all this been possible? How had Europe's most wanted man been able to escape justice for so long? Where had he been hiding? Who had been protecting him? It was believed by some that he had made a deal with the Americans ... or with the French ... or with the British. There were rumours that he had been living in a monastery disguised as a priest; or that he had spent time hiding in remote caves in the Bosnian mountains.

What was the truth? Where had Radovan Karadžić been, and how had he avoided his pursuers for so long?

1

Baptism of Fire

'A woman stood up, shouting and yelling. A grieving boy,
in religious dress, was standing by the white tombstone,
screaming, "I was a witness! I was a witness!" But was
anyone listening?' – Diary excerpt, 11 July 2002

There is a valley in Bosnia-Herzegovina, off the beaten track
and away from prying eyes, which is surrounded by sheer cliffs
and soaring mountains. A narrow, bubbling stream, clear and
fresh, cuts through it. From its banks steep slopes rise through
orchards and lush grass, eventually giving way to the rock and
scrub of the higher reaches. In secret mountain fissures, rock
pools support rare species of plant and fish. On the remote
clifftops eagles nest. It is even said that bears roam the forests,
though I have never seen any.

At the entrance to the valley there is a great tooth of rock,
slightly crooked and crumbling, standing sentinel. Carved into
its weather-beaten face is an inscription. Although it is written
in *bosančica*, a long-extinct Bosnian script, its words and their
meaning are still known.

It is a warning to travellers. It tells them they must not
harm, spoil or defile this beautiful, hidden place. If they do,
they will be doomed to suffer punishment for all eternity.
The text was written some time in the Middle Ages, but the
warning has been ignored from that day to this. War and
destruction have been frequent visitors. And, just like the
valley, Bosnia has not been able to protect itself from man's

self-destructiveness. Indeed, I sometimes think that those words were not really written as a warning but rather as a prophecy of what was to come. Perhaps it was this beautiful country's fateful vulnerability that was finally luring me back.

The high-pitched roar of the jet engines slowed gradually to a halt. The doors of the Lufthansa plane opened and, before I knew it, I was walking across the burning tarmac to the small terminal building at Sarajevo airport. It was before noon in mid-summer and the sun was riding high. I collected all my worldly possessions from the rudimentary, but working, conveyor belt in Arrivals – four black bin liners stuffed with clothes, three medium-sized suitcases, and a collection of files and books – and struggled to a waiting taxi.

I had arranged to rent a flat halfway up one of the hills surrounding the city. The view was spectacular, and that first night I remember watching a thunderstorm rage over Trebevic mountain across the valley, as if to mark my arrival. From my window I could see the three buildings representing the religions of Bosnia: the mosque, the Serbian Orthodox church and the Catholic cathedral. Clouds and lightning danced between them, but all of them were soaked in the same grey rain. I put my books on the former Yugoslavia into a book-case then gazed out of the window, watching the storm.

This was not my first time in Bosnia. Three years previously, in 1999, I had been in the country to do a story about returning refugees. It had been a facility trip arranged by the British Army, keen to show journalists what a good job they were doing in post-war Bosnia. An RAF Hercules transport plane had dropped me at a base in neighbouring Croatia and, along with an armed escort and a van filled with winter clothes and rations, we had trekked over the snow-covered mountains into Bosnia. We crossed old battlefields littered with the carcasses of burnt-out tanks; battle-scarred village after village with roofless abandoned buildings peppered with bullet holes. It was the first war zone, or rather ex-war zone, I had ever visited. As we passed through the villages we saw people drinking coffee or queuing at bus stops or making their way to school. It seemed strangely normal, the inhabitants apparently oblivious to the fact that four years previously this place had witnessed one of the most destructive wars of the twentieth century.

At one point on the road, my media minder turned to me and said: 'You know something, Nick?' affecting a pause, to emphasise the importance of what he was about to say. 'They're all the same here – totally mad! They've been killing each other for centuries. Did you know that in the old Yugoslavia, every schoolboy and schoolgirl was taught how to fire a gun and make a bomb? Is it any wonder they all end up killing each other?' He looked out of the window and sighed, content that he had just given me the one and only history lesson I would ever need to understand this part of the world. Of course, it was just another Balkan myth, but I was too innocent to know that then.

The trip lasted less than a week but, by the end, I was hooked. It was the middle of a Bosnian winter with temperatures frequently hitting −30° at night. Forests clung to the sides of mountains, naked and black. Rivers, and there were many, froze into silence. The roads were treacherous, often impassable. But there was something appealing to me about the sheer rawness of the environment. Bosnia is a wilderness, sparsely populated, and it is in winter that you feel it most. Still, I met enough people and heard enough stories, both recent and ancient, to become fascinated by the country. It was a place I wanted to come back to and explore further.

I had spent the next three years working as a political reporter in Westminster. But the chimes of Big Ben and the mystique of the Palace of Westminster had gradually faded. The lure of the Balkans had grown and now, finally, I'd returned. The BBC had, to all intents and purposes, closed down its Bosnia operation. The death and destruction were over and the organisation's resources had been reallocated. In the fickle world of international news, Bosnia was simply no longer a current story. I would have no bureau, no producer, no car, no phone, no cameraman. I had been warned as much by my predecessor in a handover meeting a few weeks earlier. She had told me there would be minimal support from London barring business cards and, maybe, a first aid kit. Despite the glamorous image of foreign news journalism, she had travelled to do stories by bus or by tram or, if she got lucky, by hitching a ride with someone from an international organisation like the UN. She had bought her own tape recorder to use for interviews.

So it was going to be foreign news on a shoestring. My office would be my flat. My equipment would be what I could afford to buy or what I could beg from others. The good news was that because Bosnia was not big news any more, London would be less demanding about the stories it required from me. Which meant I would have the freedom to pursue those that interested me most.

It was my first foreign posting. I felt energised and enthused by what lay ahead, and gradually I fell in love with the city that had become my home. I liked the mosques and churches, the bridges and coffee shops. I liked the Turkish quarter, the Austro-Hungarian quarter, and the modern suburb of Grbavica with its tree-lined streets. And I liked the fact that you could explore everywhere on foot because everything was so close. I liked the people: their laughter, friendliness, warmth. I liked the conspiracy theories that everyone had, and I liked my ex-basketball player landlord who loved to play chess but would never finish building my flat. I even liked the dodgy gangsters at the bottom of the street with their flash cars and flashier smiles.

In those first few weeks I met many people who gave me their own take on the situation in Bosnia. I had lunch with a foreign diplomat at a restaurant called Hunter. As he scoffed his squid and potato lunch, he told me the do's and don'ts of Sarajevo life. Do accept all hospitality that is offered. Don't fall into the trap of believing what you read in the papers. Do remember that the only thing that is respected here is strength. Then, as he devoured his fruit salad at the same phenomenal rate as he'd dealt with the squid and potato, he paused for just a moment before offering a final piece of advice: 'The key thing is to be able to separate fact from fiction. Or, as I like to say, be able to "remove the froth". Nothing else matters.'

After wiping his face with a less-than-clean napkin, he took his leave. At least he paid the bill.

Then there was my trip to meet the Bosnian President's spokesman. I entered the Presidency building through what appeared to be a fire escape but was in fact the main door. Having passed through the unattended metal detector and drifted around the corridors of state without let or hindrance for a good twenty minutes, I eventually found the office. The dolly-bird assistant, fag in hand, denim jacket on back of chair and hairspray in hand, guided me into a cavernous office. At the far end was the spokesman, casual in shirt and slippers. Apart from a desk, two chairs and one plant, the room was empty. We drank coffee and orange juice. For half an hour he plied me with the rhetoric of Bosnian politics. Finally he patted me on the back, gave me a beaming smile and handed me a book. By the time I was outside in the fresh air, the substance of what he had said was already a distant memory. Suffice it to say, my first experience at the heart of the Bosnian political system was less than enlightening.

A week later, my landlord took me on a drive up Trebevic mountain. Before the war, the woodland and pathways of Trebevic had been popular with Sarajevans. But since the guns had fallen silent, an eerie sense of desolation had descended. Few now made that short trip up the mountain. It was the first time in 13 years that my landlord had been here. 'It was from here that they shelled or shot at us. This was where death came from,' he told me by way of explanation.

As the road wound its way upwards, I could see the trees, their upper branches shot away, a graphic reminder of the fighting. Trenches and sandbags littered the slopes. Signs indicating minefields appeared every few metres. The only person we passed was a shepherd. At one point, we got out of the car and looked down on Sarajevo below. It appeared so close, I could easily make out the streets and individual buildings.

Half a million people below, one shepherd above, and all in the space of a ten-minute car journey.

I knew how Sarajevo and its people had suffered, and not just in the recent past. In the twentieth century alone, the city had seen one war, then another, then another, and finally, in the 1990s, one of the worst. There was not a building without either bullet or shell hole. Sarajevo had suffered the longest siege in modern history, three and a half years, longer even than Leningrad's. Someone had said it was the only place in the world where everyone was suffering from some form of post-traumatic stress. Half the city had trees, the other half did not, because those living within the siege area had had to chop them down for firewood since there was no other source of heating.

And then there were the less obvious forms of damage. Close to the gangsters lived a blonde woman – I only ever knew her as that. She was not unattractive: in her thirties, always well dressed, her hair neat and styled, intelligent eyes. But she was always alone. I never saw her with or even talking to anyone. I never saw her shopping or driving or really going anywhere. Sometimes she would start walking then turn back. Occasionally she would mumble something to herself. But I never caught the words. Usually I saw her sitting at the window of her ground-floor flat, just staring out. I never saw her cry. I never saw her angry. I never saw her laugh or smile. I never saw joy or sadness in her face. Something had snapped inside her. For this woman, all meaning had gone from life. And she was not the only one.

My conversations with people almost always contained one of two phrases: '*prije rata*'; or '*poslje rata*'; 'before the war' or 'after the war'. Whatever the subject or whoever was talking, everything was defined, everything contextualised, by one of these two phrases. 'How much were those bananas you just bought from the market?' asks Aida 'Well, they were quite cheap really, but they were cheaper before the war,' replies Dragana. Or another conversation: 'Have you heard about that robbery down the street?' says Almir. 'Yes,' says Igor, 'it's got a lot worse after the war. Before, we used to have a good, strong police force.' It really was like that – everything and everyone defined by their relationship to the war.

And there were the subtleties of suffering that I just did not see, at least not in those early days. The smile that was not really a smile, just a way of avoiding talking about the pain; a watery eye averted before I saw it; the slight tremor in the voice before it was covered with a cough. It took some time before I saw and understood those signs.

But then, one day, I witnessed suffering in its rawest and most candid form. I will never forget it. I had been in the Bosnian capital less than a month when I made my first trip into the 'badlands', as some people called them. Through a contact of a contact, I presented myself at the plush offices of an international news agency in Sarajevo. After a little cajoling, I managed to get a spare seat in one of their cars that was making a trip to the east of the country. It was 11 July 2002 and the seventh anniversary of the most notorious event of the Bosnian War: the Srebrenica massacre.

Of all the subjects that could generate passion and anger among the people of post-war Bosnia, it was the subject of Srebrenica, the town in eastern Bosnia where, in July 1995, Serb forces had systematically murdered 8,000 Muslim men and boys in an unprecedented orgy of violence. Over the years, the Serb authorities had made all sorts of claims in order to diminish the scale of the crime: that 'only' 2,000 had been killed; that they had all died fighting among themselves; that they had all committed suicide; that they were soldiers justifiably killed in combat; even that President Clinton had ordered the killings.

But there were two major problems with all of these arguments: first were the damning television pictures from 1995 which clearly showed Serb troops separating the men from the women outside the UN compound at Potočari, close to Srebrenica; and, secondly, every year, more mass graves containing the remains of those who had been killed were being discovered. These would usually appear in the spring when the winter snows melted and the water gradually shifted soil and rock. Human remains would appear and another forgotten pit of death would emerge into the sunlight, disclosing the bodies of the victims and, in turn, disclosing the lie.

It was just after dawn when we set off but already the sky was clear and the sun was bright. This was my first trip into the east, into the heart of the Serb-dominated region of the country.

The war had left Bosnia, one of the former six republics making up Yugoslavia (along with Serbia, Croatia, Slovenia, Montenegro and Macedonia), as an independent state. But Bosnia itself was divided into two armed camps: the Republika Srpska, which was dominated by the Serbs, and the Muslim-Croat Federation, which was dominated by the Muslims and Croats. Both so-called entities had all the characteristics of mini-states, with their own governments, parliaments, armies and police forces. Sarajevo was the capital of the country and the Federation but Srebrenica was in the Republika Srpska.

The journey was breathtaking, passing through pine forests and over mountain passes, crossing rivers and streams, the narrow road adding to the feeling of inaccessibility and isolation. There were spectacular views east from Romanija mountain towards Serbia in the distance. The outstanding natural beauty of the country seduced me once again.

Tito had not only recognised the beauty but also the military potential of such an environment. He turned Bosnia into Yugoslavia's last redoubt, furnishing it with an arms industry and countless secret underground military facilities. If the Warsaw Pact or NATO had ever decided to invade, then it would have been to Bosnia that Yugoslavia's leadership would have fled. They would have relied on the mountains and forests to hide them and on guerrilla tactics to repel the invaders – just as Tito's Partisans had done during the Second World War.

We were not the only ones making the journey that morning.

In July every year the widows, relatives and friends of those who had died returned to Srebrenica, not merely to pay their respects to the dead but also to continue to press for more to be done to trace the remains of missing loved ones. We crossed into the Republika Srpska. A decade ago this line had been in no man's land with heavily armed forces poised on either side. But now the border was marked by nothing more than a large sign. Next to the road gushed a river lined with twisted trees, heavy with white blossom. If it had not been for the thousands of plastic bags that had wrapped themselves around the lower branches close to the water – a bizarre feature of many Bosnian rivers – it could have been a tourist hotspot.

As we entered the Serb-controlled area, I tensed a little. Almost immediately we saw a Bosnian Serb policeman, in light blue uniform with a pistol at his side, standing by the road. And then another. And another. In fact, the whole country road was lined with Serb policemen standing 50 metres or so apart. We were far away from any village or town, in the middle of the Bosnian wilderness, and yet here were policemen seemingly forming a loose cordon along the road. They looked uninterested, reluctant to be here. I asked my colleague what they were doing and he told me they had to guard the road because the widows and friends of those who had died at Srebrenica would soon be travelling along it on the way to the commemoration. The authorities could not take the chance that some disgruntled local Serb would take a pot shot at the passing vehicles. The line of policemen stretched down the road, kilometre after kilometre. We began to pass some of the coaches on their way to Srebrenica. I could see the women wearing the traditional, colourful Muslim headscarves. Some were in tears, others were just staring out of the window.

After two hours we reached the small town of Bratunac. The main street had obviously seen better days, with its broken traffic lights, cracked pavements and scruffy low-rise buildings. The place looked forlorn, half-abandoned, like a town at the end of the world. But today was a special day. The locals had come out into the streets to watch the arrival of the buses. They were Serbs. The Muslims had been expelled a long time ago, during the war, and they did not want to see them back. Their faces were rigid with anger.

Our car slowed to a crawl as the traffic was squeezed by a Serbian police diversion into the narrow back streets. NATO helicopters were circling above, monitoring the crowds. We ended up in a convoy with the coaches carrying the relatives. The local people standing on the pavements, just metres away, were jeering and raising clenched fists as the coaches slowly passed by. There were old men and young children, husbands and wives, many waving Serbian flags. There was hatred and fury in their eyes. I saw a boy, no older than three, waving a pistol at the coach in front of me. I thought it was a plastic gun but, thinking back now, I cannot be sure. Others held posters of former Bosnian Serb wartime leaders, thrusting them into the air as the vehicles passed. They shouted obscenities at the people on the coaches and spat at the windows. I was shocked by the whole scene. So much hatred from so many people, concentrated in such a small place.

We turned towards Potočari, the village between Bratunac and Srebrenica where, in 1995, thousands of refugees had gathered, hoping to find sanctuary with the small UN Dutch military contingent garrisoned in the town. But their hopes were in vain. The Serbs easily overpowered the lightly armed Dutch and the general leading the Bosnian Serbs, Ratko Mladić, was shown on television approaching the UN base with a smile on his face, looking for all the world as if he were just out on a Sunday afternoon walk. In the days that followed, thousands of Muslim men and boys were slaughtered by Mladić's forces in fields and buildings in the surrounding countryside.

Now, across the road from the old UN base, a huge memorial cemetery was being built in honour of those who had been killed. It was basically just a large field with gently rising slopes at the far end. The cemetery's boundaries were being marked out in such a way that the whole area would ultimately form the shape of the petals of a flower. Beyond, Serb houses overlooked the construction. The aim in the long term was to have a grave for every one of the Srebrenica victims, more than 8,000 white Muslim tombstones. But that depended on whether all the victims would ever be found.

The temperature was in the mid 30s and there was no shelter from the sun unless you were one of the invited VIPs allocated a place under the specially erected marquee. The tent itself was surrounded by the VIPs' bodyguards, sporting their shiny sunglasses and designer earpieces and fingering their semi-automatics. In total contrast, the widows, now released from the cramped and airless coaches, were crouching or sitting on the grass slopes of the cemetery, with only their headscarves for protection from the sun. Some of them were drinking from water bottles and unwrapping sandwiches made for the day.

The ceremony, led by an imam, was conducted in the sweltering afternoon heat. He stood near a single white marble tombstone that was a symbolic representation of all the victims. Speakers relayed his words around the field and up the slopes. There were 3,000 people here to listen to the prayers for the dead. I did not understand most of the words but at one point I heard the name 'Martin Luther King' and realised that the American civil rights leader was being quoted, for one reason or another. The VIPs, from the West and from Bosnia, standing under their awnings, looked serious and sad and concerned, all at the same time. The speeches and praying were finally over. The crowd dispersed, but I watched as some of the women remained sitting in small groups, saying little, crying a lot. The VIPs drifted off to their big cars and their big escorts. The tension ebbed away.

There had been a lot of emotion, a lot of sorrow. But when I thought about it, I realised that there had been no real anger. Everything had remained incredibly dignified. There had been no calls for revenge, and no animosity had been shown by the thousands of mourners despite the proximity of so many Serb policemen, some of whom, it was rumoured, may even have been in Srebrenica during those dark days.

The widows began to stand up and walk slowly back to the car park across the road where their coaches were waiting. I began to pack my things and think about looking for my colleagues whom I had lost in the crowd. And then I heard it: a voice crying and shouting at the same time, somewhere ahead of me. I moved through the thinning crowd towards the noise. A boy of about 14 was standing alone, dressed in a light-coloured cloak. I switched on my microphone and moved closer. He was standing where the imam had been, next to the tombstone. I looked at the boy's face. His bottom teeth were broken and bent. His eyes were screwed up tight, tears streaming down his face. He was talking to the stone as if it were a person.

He was shouting, in Bosnian, 'I was a witness! I was a witness!' There were other sentences but I did not understand them. I kept watching and listening. He kept screaming, 'I was a witness! I was a witness!' And then, a few moments later, I heard another word. And there was no doubt what it was. He shouted the name 'Karadžić'. And then again, 'Karadžić!' I looked around at the rest of the crowd. They were staring at the boy as well. Gradually, his voice gave way and he fell to his knees, sobbing. The last remaining people drifted away. I followed them.

As I was leaving the cemetery, a man approached me. He was in his fifties, I thought, but I already knew that people here could look older than they really were. He was slightly bent but there was a spring in his step which was something rare on this saddest of days. He asked me how I was, what I had been doing. He said it had been quite a while since he had seen me. He seemed to think he knew me from some previous encounter, though I was convinced I had never seen him before. After some confused conversation and lots of smiles, it transpired that he had mistaken me for another Western journalist who had been in Srebrenica a few years earlier. They had looked for graves together. This man was a Muslim and he was called Reuf. He had moved back to the Srebrenica area and was part of the small Muslim community that, for some reason, had gradually returned to this tragic land, to live with the ghosts of their families. I gave the man my card and told him to ring me if ever he thought I should know of something that was going on in the area.

We left Potočari when the sun was setting. Once more, we braved the rows of enraged local Serbs whose ranks seemed to have thinned slightly. Perhaps their anger had waned as the day wore on. Anyway, I was not sorry to see the back of the place. On our return the road was again lined with policemen. Now I understood why. We left Republika Srpska and crossed back into the Federation at Kladanj. We stopped for a late lunch at the Motel America, a huge white complex on the main road between Tuzla and Sarajevo. My photographer colleagues were already there, filing and smoking and sipping coffee. Working for various international agencies, their images of the day were already downloaded from camera to computer and on their way to offices in London, Paris and New York. Within the hour they would be picked up by newspapers and news websites around the world.

It was late when we arrived back in Sarajevo. I picked up some *cevapi* (or traditional minced meat sausages) from one of the takeaway shops in Baščaršija, the Turkish part of town. While I queued, I watched a group of Polish tourists roaming the cobbled streets with smiles on their faces and cameras in their hands. Visitors were slowly starting to return to this blighted part of Europe, enjoying the historical sites and sampling the local cuisine.

But, lying in bed that night, there was only one image in my mind: the boy at the stone, with his rotten teeth and lines etched prematurely into his young face, and the words he'd uttered with such bitterness. I had listened again to the recording I had made of his voice and got a friend to translate it. The boy was saying many things, but there was one theme he kept returning to, one question he kept repeating: the man who had caused all this suffering, why was he still free? Why had he not been arrested? Why was Radovan Karadžić, former President of the Republika Srpska and head of the army that had carried out the killings and buried the evidence, not behind bars and facing justice?

He was asking the great unanswered question of post-war Bosnia. Along with around 20 others, including General Mladić, Radovan Karadžić was still on the run from the United Nations War Crimes Tribunal in The Hague. The issue hung like a big, dark cloud over the country. There were all sorts of rumours circulating Sarajevo. It was claimed a deal had been done to protect him from prosecution. It was claimed that no one wanted him arrested because he might reveal embarrassing secrets about the war. Some even suggested the very people and organisations that were supposed to be hunting him were, in fact, the ones protecting him.

Seven years after the Bosnian War had ended, Radovan Karadžić, the Bosnian Serb President who had dominated the country and the region for so long, whose image and voice had been ever-present on television screens and radio airwaves around the world, who had played a crucial role in a devastating war in which more than 100,000 people had been killed and 2,000,000 made homeless, had simply vanished.

Thousands of international soldiers had been stationed in Bosnia for several years. Western intelligence services had been operating in the country with virtual carte blanche. International officials had been in virtual control of Bosnia's legal and judicial framework since the war had ended. And yet Radovan Karadžić was still free.

2

Connections

> 'It's only when you switch on the light, what I call the
> "infra-red light", that you get to understand the real
> connections between people: where their loyalties really
> lie, what really motivates people, why people really do
> what they do' – Advice from a friend, October 2002

His blue eyes kept glancing over my shoulder towards the door
whenever a new customer came into the hotel bar. For a
moment, his fingers would stop spinning the orange-coloured
mobile phone which he had left on the table in front of him.
When he realised there was no threat, he would relax again,
focus on me and resume his spinning of the phone. I would
have left the hotel bar long ago, but his bizarre story kept me
enthralled. I knew this man had been involved in a thousand
operations carried out in the shadows. He was a keeper of
secrets and people feared what he knew. He had worked in
the security structures of Bosnia for most of his life.

An hour previously, my car had crunched into the snow-
covered car park of the hotel. It was winter, 2002. It was already
dark and well below freezing. My interpreter and I slipped and
stumbled as we walked towards the building and the warmth
and light inside. But neither of us could fail to notice the man
sitting in a car a few metres away, his eyes trained on us.

As we entered the bar, a man rose from a table near the
window and beckoned to us. He was slightly built, with neat
brown hair, and was wearing an anonymous brown jacket and

trousers. His handshake was warm and his smile reassuring. We sat down and ordered drinks. I had tracked down the man after spotting his name in one of the local newspapers. He was an experienced operator. He had prospered during the Communist Tito era, had watched Yugoslavia collapse, and survived the war and the turmoil that came in its wake during the 1990s. He had recently left the intelligence service and I was hoping he might be able to share some of what he knew regarding the Karadžić case.

I started off by asking some general questions to break the ice. He did not hold back. Within minutes I was hearing about secret deals, international conspiracies and Islamic terrorism. These were stories which seemed to come straight out of the pages of James Bond novels. I was told about Serbian agents allegedly trying to infiltrate international organisations in Bosnia; wives of Western diplomats who were also working for Serbia; foreign governments which were secretly supporting the nationalist political parties in Bosnia. A close wartime ally of Radovan Karadžić had been on the payroll of the British intelligence service. The French had been involved in dodgy dealings in order to win a lucrative contract for a radar system. Finally he told me that these days he was doing some work for the Prosecutor's Office in The Hague. I asked him directly about Karadžić. There seemed to be every conspiracy theory under the sun.

'It's simple. They just don't want him arrested. They want to keep the status quo here,' he said. I asked him who 'they' were. He named the High Representative for Bosnia and Herzegovina, Paddy Ashdown, and several leading Muslim politicians. 'The Muslims don't want him arrested because they believe they could be the next ones to go to The Hague. Ashdown doesn't want him arrested because the foreigners need a reason to stay in Bosnia to do other things.'

'What other things?'

'There is a lot of interest these days in tracking down Muslim extremists. I know where Karadžić is. I was about twenty days away from launching an operation to capture him myself when

I was forced to leave my job. That is why they got rid of me. If you do not believe me, ask The Hague. I have been working for them. Ask Del Ponte. She will tell you'.

I asked him for details, for the location of the former Bosnian Serb leader now, but he would say no more.

As we left the bar, my interpreter pointed to three men at a nearby table. 'They've been watching us the whole time,' he whispered out of the corner of his mouth. 'They were making signals to the man we were talking to.' I half turned towards the men at the table. I thought one of them was the man we had seen sitting in the parked car when we arrived. But who were they . . . bodyguards . . . police?

As we drove back to Sarajevo, I was not sure what to believe. Intriguingly, my contact had suggested that the Chief Prosecutor at The Hague, Carla Del Ponte, might be able to confirm some of his claims. For the past three years, Del Ponte, a diminutive blonde lawyer from Switzerland with staring eyes behind severe dark-framed glasses, had been pursuing the former Yugoslavia's most wanted men. She had established her hard-line persona by first fighting the Sicilian Mafia. But there were rumours that, in her eagerness to track down Karadžić and Mladić, she had ruffled quite a few feathers in the international community. In fact, her relations with some officials were said to be 'shaky' at best. Part of the problem was that The Hague Tribunal had acquired something of a mixed reputation, especially in the former Yugoslavia. Some saw it simply as a political institution, administering a victor's justice. Others, who saw its potential value, were disillusioned by the time-scale of the trials it conducted.*

On a practical level, the court, or rather the prosecution element of it, had very few powers and resources. It did not have any special police teams who could go and carry out

---

* The best example of this would be the trial of the former President of the Federal Republic of Yugoslavia, Slobodan Milošević. Accused of genocide, murder, ethnic cleansing, torture and extermination, he first appeared in a courtroom in The Hague in July 2001, but his trial would not even be over by the time he died of a heart attack in his cell in the UN Detention Centre in March 2006.

arrests. There was no real intelligence-gathering. It relied entirely on the good-will of the peacekeepers on the ground or the generosity of Western intelligence agencies, especially the United States and its allies. This usually came down to the personal relationships that could be established between representatives of the two sides. Above everything, The Hague Tribunal represented an entirely new concept in international justice and there were always going to be teething problems with that. The testing ground for the court could hardly have been more difficult, given the complicated post-war environment in the former Yugoslavia.

As luck would have it, a few days after my meeting in the hotel bar, Carla Del Ponte was due to arrive in Sarajevo on one of her regular visits to twist arms and try to cajole the relevant authorities to do more. I knew that she was going to the Holiday Inn and made sure I was there for her arrival.

Del Ponte's cavalcade swept into the car park of the hotel, blue lights flashing. In seconds burly bodyguards were deployed at every door and the Chief Prosecutor herself jumped out of one of the vehicles. Surrounded by advisers and bodyguards, she marched into the huge lobby of the hotel and headed to an area at the back of the ground-floor bar which was cordoned off for her.

For an hour I watched as she and a group of people sat round a table talking in hushed tones. At one point I intercepted one of her advisers on his way to the toilet and asked whether she might have time for a chat once she had finished her meeting. The grim-faced official said she would do her best but he could not promise anything.

When her meeting finished, I was quite surprised when Del Ponte came over to me. She said she could give me five minutes. Chain-smoking in front of me, she confirmed that she had been very surprised that the Bosnian spy I'd met had been forced to leave his job.

'It was a great loss to us. I complained that Lord Ashdown did not get in touch with me before taking the decision,' she said.

'He told me that one of the principle reasons for his [the spy's] removal was that he was getting close to providing information that could lead to Karadžić's arrest. Do you believe that?' I asked.

'I don't know,' she replied. 'I can only speak about what we are doing with him and what co-operation we receive from him, but I hope he was not removed for that reason.'

'Why is it, do you think, the West has not arrested Karadžić?'

'It's a good question but I have no answer, unfortunately.'

After the interview one of her advisers took me to one side and, sotto voce, suggested that I might want to continue sniffing around to find out why the agent had been relieved of his job. He would not say any more. Then the entourage swept out of the hotel for the airport, sirens wailing.

The Dayton Peace Agreement of 1995 had finally brought the bloody Bosnian War to an end. After three and a half years of atrocities, mass killings, ethnic cleansing and the abuse of human rights on a scale not seen in Europe for 50 years, observed by a divided and apparently powerless international community, peace was declared. But no long-term political solution was found, no long-term stability guaranteed. Rather, in the long term Dayton sowed the seeds of political and economic fragmentation. For a decade after the war, Bosnia-Herzegovina was, in name, a single state. In reality, it was two states in one.

The Republika Srpska and Muslim-Croat Federation not only had their own distinct political and security systems, but they also had their own tax, education and health systems. And although everyone spoke what was, essentially, the same language, Serbo-Croat, they used different alphabets: the Serbs used Cyrillic, the Muslims and Croats used Latinic. There was a very fragile state structure over-arching these two entities, with a national Parliament, Presidency and, eventually, Prime Minister. But, in reality, all power lay with the separate entities.

By 2002, if you included all the country's political structures at national and local level, Bosnia had five Presidents, 12 Prime Ministers and 13 Parliaments. There were three official religions (Islam, Serbian Orthodox and Roman Catholic), three official languages (Bosnian, Serbian and Croatian), three armies, two police forces, and two customs services. All this in a country with a population of less than 4,000,000 – though no one really knew the exact number since there had not been a census since before the war.

International organisations mushroomed in the years after 1995. There was SFOR (originally named IFOR), the NATO-led peacekeepers who at one time numbered 60,000 but whose force had dropped to around 12,000 by 2002. There was the United Nations in all its various guises: the UN Mission in Bosnia (UNMIBH); the UN Commission for Refugees (UNHCR); the UN Development Programme (UNDP). Then there was the European Union, represented by the European Commission (EC) and the European Union Monitoring Mission (EUMM). There was also the Organisation for Security and Co-operation in Europe (OSCE), the World Bank, the International Monetary Fund, the International Commission for Missing Persons (ICMP), the International Criminal Tribunal for the former-Yugoslavia (ICTY – or The Hague Tribunal). On top of all that there was a myriad of civil society groups and non-governmental organisations, working on everything from mine clearance to cat shelters.

At the top of the tree was the Office of the High Representative (OHR). This had been set up by the Peace Implementation Council, the international body charged with implementing the Dayton Peace Agreement. This was the highest political office in the country, run by an international diplomat supported by 800 staff, spread around the country. Their aim was to ensure that the civilian aspects of the Dayton Peace Agreement were carried through.

The post of High Representative was similar to that of the old colonial Governors of the British Empire. The 'High Rep', as he became known, could sack and suspend public officials and politicians, even remove Presidents and Prime Ministers from their positions. It was felt that such powers were needed in order to prevent obstruction by local authorities or particular individuals. The High Rep's job was also to co-ordinate the work of all the international organisations in Bosnia. This was no easy task. The High Rep had no formal powers to do this, with each organisation following its own mandate and reporting to its own headquarters. Co-ordination depended on the goodwill of the heads of each of these organisations and the strength of character of whoever was High Rep at the time.

By 2002, Bosnia was in political and economic limbo. The war was long since over but people's expectations had not been met. As I wandered the streets of Sarajevo, I could still see damage from the conflict on every building. There were very few signs of investment or of new jobs being created. Around the rest of the country, the picture was similar. The only major construction work that seemed to be going on was the rebuilding of ruined houses. But there were still villages you could drive through that had been totally abandoned. Some of the buildings were overgrown with trees and grass. These were the ones to avoid in case booby traps had been left behind. Bosnia was in the doldrums, held back by the incredibly complicated domestic political environment combined with the heavy presence of disparate international organisations.

The international community recognised the need for reform and began to make efforts to strengthen state structures and simplify decision-making processes. But it was going to be an uphill task. The central problem was that half of the country, the Republika Srpska, simply did not want to see the creation of a single state. The Serbs had fought the war because they had not wanted to be part of an independent Bosnia. They could see no reason to change their minds now. Many of the Muslim and Croat leaders in the other half of the country also had their own reasons to delay the process of reform. Some of them had established their own fiefdoms, power bases and sources of wealth since the war had ended, and were in no rush to give these up. Political leaders in all parts of the country were also believed to have links to organised crime and corruption so there was an added incentive to maintain the status quo. While the international community struggled to bring 'democratisation', 'human rights' and 'reconciliation' to Bosnia through an unprecedented number of programmes and projects, many people were happy to take the money and support, but to do little else. Avoiding both political responsibility and accountability became an art form for many local politicians.

One of the first things that the international community did once the war was over was to hold elections. Not surprisingly, all ethnic groups simply re-elected their wartime leaders and political parties, and these leaders maintained or reappointed their own politicians and generals. So, effectively, the wartime power structures were perpetuated. Although there were 60,000 peacekeepers in place and an international civilian administrator with powers to oversee the implementation of the peace agreement, no attempt was made to clean up the Augean stables. And there was no clear line of responsibility on the issue of war criminals. The international community insisted it was the job of the local security structures to track down the fugitives, but what chance was there of that when the people in power were often the friends and allies of the very people being sought?

The General Framework Agreement (Dayton Peace Agreement) called on all sides to:

> ... co-operate fully with all entities involved in implementation of this peace settlement, as described in the General Framework Agreement, or which are otherwise authorised by the United Nations Security Council, including the International Tribunal for the Former Yugoslavia.

This was wishful thinking. The Military Annex to Dayton only:

> ... authorise[d] the IFOR [Implementation Force] to take such actions as required, including the use of necessary force, to ensure compliance with this Annex, and to ensure its own protection.

The unwillingness of local security structures to carry out arrests, coupled with a lack of clear instruction to NATO peacemakers, in effect gave war criminals a head start. When the internationals finally decided to join the hunt, the criminals were long gone.

Radovan Karadžić was born on 19 June 1945, just days after the end of World War II in Europe. He was born in north-west Montenegro, in a half-destroyed house, in the shadow of a mountain called Soldier. At the time, only two buildings in the village were left standing; the rest had been razed to the ground. The only water available came from a spring near the village and there was no electricity. Like others in the village seeking shelter, the Karadžić family had scraped out a hollow on a grass slope, surrounded it with a few stones and laid a rudimentary roof on top. There was little else that could be done. Today, amidst the wild apple and pear trees, you can still see a few of the stones which mark the place where the future President was born.

The Karadžić family had lived in the village of Petnica for centuries, as testified by the Karadžić gravestones in the local churchyard. Family legend has it that the clan originally came from Karadžića mountain in today's former Yugoslav Republic of Macedonia but were forced to move as the Ottoman Empire expanded further north into the Balkans. The family finally settled in Petnica near the town of Nikšić in north-west Montenegro in the mid-seventeenth century. The Karadžićs are said to have been led by three brothers who rose to be leaders of the local community during the resistance to the Ottomans.

The Ottoman Empire controlled most of the Balkans for 500 years until it imploded at the end of the nineteenth century. Further destabilisation and conflict occurred in the region during the power vacuum after the Empire's demise. Many of the attitudes and prejudices that are rife among the peoples of the Balkans today are a direct result of their experiences under the Ottomans.

The Ottomans never quite conquered the whole of Montenegro. This was either because of the fierce resistance they encountered or simply because they had no strategic need to possess the mountainous and barren interior of this part of the Balkans. Whatever the case, there is evident local pride in places like Petnica over their defiance of the all-conquering

Turk. On one of the hills above the village, there is the so-called 'Turkish graveyard' where some of the victims of the resistance are buried, their belongings and riches long since plundered. There are many mountainside memorials to past battles between the invaders and the local population. The Karadžićs saw themselves as leaders in the fight to defend the Serbian Orthodox religion, to oppose Turkish taxation, and what they saw as the Islamisation of the area.

The Ottoman Empire's final death throes in the Balkans did not occur until 1912–13 with the so-called Balkan Wars when regional states, including Montenegro, sought to win their freedom from the ailing empire. More than a year of fighting took place as Bulgaria, Serbia, Greece and Montenegro engaged in separate battles against the Ottomans, and, ultimately, each other. The end result was that the Ottomans were finally expelled and the political borders re-drawn. But the cycle of violence which would characterise much of the twentieth century was only just beginning.

On June 28 1914 Archduke Franz Ferdinand, heir to the Austro-Hungarian throne, was assassinated in Sarajevo, heralding the start of World War I. As the great powers slugged it out on the mud-caked battle-fields of Western Europe, the Balkans experienced its own sideshow of horror and massacre, this time with the Austrians playing the role of new Imperial invaders. Four years later, they found themselves on the losing side. But the ensuing relative peace and stability in the Balkans were to be short-lived. In April 1941 Hitler's bombers attacked Belgrade and the Axis powers dispatched their armies to occupy much of the Balkans.

The Germans and Italians divided up the conquered territory into separate zones. The area around Petnica was given to the Italians. Three Italian divisions entered Montenegro on 17 April 1941. Eventually, 10,000 Italian troops would be stationed in 20 garrisons in the area. An uprising against the Italians began on 13 July 1941 – although, according to Karadžić family folklore, the village of Petnica rose up even before this date. Two main resistance groups emerged: the Četniks or royalists, whose loyalty was to the King of Yugoslavia, and the Partisans, led by the Communist Josip 'Broz' Tito. These two groups would ultimately fight each other.

In Petnica, of the 50 or so male residents, the majority were royalists, including the Karadžićs. The uprising was initially successful, but the Italians soon responded with reinforcements. In April 1942 30 members of the Karadžić clan were executed in nearby Šavnik.

Over the next three years the region witnessed a complex series of struggles between Germans, Italians, Fascist Croats, Partisans and Četniks, all vying for supremacy over the mountains, valleys and plains of Yugoslavia. The fighting was brutal and quarter rarely given. The Germans and their allies launched a number of offensives to try to wipe out Tito's Partisans and other opposition forces. It was during the so-called German Fifth Offensive of May 1943 that Petnica was razed to the ground. Only the church and one house remained standing. The cattle were taken, possessions destroyed or looted, the people left homeless.

By September 1945 virtually everyone in the village of Petnica was living in single-room dug-outs in the ground, covered with tarpaulin. Life was hard, the future uncertain. The Partisans were now in power. The war had divided families and communities. Thousand upon thousand had been killed – no one really knew how many. The Karadžićs had fought on the side of the Četniks. The question now was whether the victorious Tito would launch a purge against those who had opposed him.

Some of the men were wearing Karadžić and Mladić T-shirts. They were chanting Serbian nationalist songs in the heart of Sarajevo. Clapping their hands and jumping up and down, the 200 Yugoslav (Serbia and Montenegro continued to call themselves Yugoslavia at this time) football fans had come to watch their team play Bosnia in the first-ever match between the two countries. Their provocations were matched by the home fans who were waving Turkish and Islamic flags. With violence anticipated, I had come to report on the event rather than the game. In the cold night air, the setting could hardly have been more dramatic: an Olympic Stadium, surrounded by mountains and a huge cemetery crammed with the dead from the last war.

After the match, which Yugoslavia won, hundreds of Bosnian fans tried to storm the terraces where the Serb fans were congregated. I was caught in the middle as riot police kept the two sides apart. Bottles, bricks, signposts . . . everything that came to hand was used in the mêlée. I retreated to a doorway as the riot police charged. A few dozen people were injured, a couple seriously. Numerous arrests were made. A wizened old hack standing nearby muttered, 'It could have been a lot worse.'

A few days later, in an outdoor cafe in the Turkish quarter of the city, I received my first practical lesson in the difficulties of trying to separate fact from fiction, or 'removing the froth' as the diplomat had called it. I was establishing my first contact with the international peacekeepers. One man had expressed an interest in meeting me, as the new journalist in town. I took the opportunity to ask him if I would be able to accompany the next peacekeeping raid to arrest a war crimes fugitive, especially if it was Karadžić. He was non-committal. After our coffee, he left the cafe and I started writing up my notes. A few minutes, later my phone rang. It was my contact.

'I was just wondering, are you going on vacation soon?' he asked

'Yes, as a matter of fact. I was about to book something.'

'Well, you might want to cancel it.'

'Why's that?'

'It might be a good idea to stay in town for the next two weeks. Could be worth your while.'

He would not say more. I took this as a clear signal that an arrest operation for Karadžić was to be launched some time in the next few days. Excited by the prospect, I contacted my editors in London, informing them of the tip-off. Contingency measures were put in place. For two weeks I sat by the phone waiting for a call from my contact. It never came.

The Romanian hooker looked at me and said she spoke four languages: Romanian, English, Spanish and Bosnian. Which one did I want her to speak? She lay on a mattress on the floor in a room filled with other mattresses, Coke cans, cigarette packs and condoms. She was 24, smiling, apparently happy, and just a little annoyed that we had raided the place. At the door, on the stairs and in the ground-floor bar, men carrying shotguns, dressed in black with balaclavas over their heads, stood guard.

It was late-November, not long after my meeting with the

Bosnian spy. I was on a raid with a Bosnian special police unit and members of the UN's police force. We were raiding bars, or rather brothels, in search of trafficked women. I was there to do a report about the latest crackdown. In this particular place, not far from Sarajevo, no trafficked women were found and the only international customer was a shy Turkish businessman.

A few minutes earlier we had arrived with flashing lights and screeching tyres. As the men in balaclavas jumped out of their cars, a man left the bar and calmly walked to his black Mercedes. A couple of the special policemen went over to speak to him, then they saluted and the Mercedes reversed slowly out of the car park and drove away. One of the international policemen who was watching the incident grimaced.

'Look at that,' he said. 'They are meant to do full searches, ask for documents. Not let them just drive away. But what can we do? It's too late now.' Whichever bar we raided that night, it seemed that the usual clientele had been forewarned. No trafficked women were found, no arrests were made.

This was a small country with small communities. In many places everyone knew everyone else. It was difficult to be anonymous. There was always a way of finding someone or of knowing someone else's business. As a result, it was almost impossible to know what was really motivating people and what loyalties they really had. During my first few months in Sarajevo, an experienced old international had taken me to one side and explained how I should try to understand things.

'You see, it's like this. In Western countries, society and power are generally based on vertical structures. There is the boss, director, manager or police chief. After this, lower down, comes the deputy or official. Below that is the worker, the administrator. The most power is at the top and it is delegated downwards.

'Here, it is different. Sure, on the surface there are vertical structures and chains of command, but in reality everything is different. Switch on the infra-red light and you see the real power, the real connections, the real structures. The police chief might be married to a shopkeeper whose uncle is the Minister. Or the low-level government official's cousin's auntie is the big crime boss whose best friend is the Minister for the Interior, and so on and so on. It is these horizontal connections you need to understand if you want to understand Bosnia.

'Of course, when you switch the infra-red light off, all those normal, vertical structures, with their natural lines of command and power and connection are back again and no one is any the wiser. You need to have the infra-red switched on the whole time. That is the only way to understand who has power and how it is really exercised.'

For several years after 1995 the nationalists on all sides held the levers of power. There was no single international organisation dedicated to capturing war criminals – only the International Criminal Tribunal for the former Yugoslavia. But the ICTY had neither mandate nor resources to carry out its own arrest operations. The Tribunal was entirely in the hands of the local institutions, national intelligence agencies or the peacekeepers.

In July 1997 the situation changed dramatically when British Special Forces attempted to arrest two Bosnian Serb war crimes fugitives wanted by the ICTY in northern Bosnia. One of the accused was killed in the ensuing shoot-out. The other was arrested. Over the years more operations were carried out and more cells were occupied at The Hague Tribunal. But it was a haphazard process and progress was slow, especially when it came to the most high-ranking individuals like Karadžić and Mladić. As one security source put it: 'There was a fundamental mistake early on. They started picking the fruit off the lower branches of the tree first. That gave a warning to the fruit higher up the tree who then had time to make their plans and go into deeper hiding.'

It was not until February 2002 that any serious operation was mounted to arrest Karadžić himself when hundreds of SFOR (Stabilisation Force, taking over from Implementation

Force) descended on a remote area of south-east Bosnia near the village of Čelebići. Roads and villages were sealed off as NATO helicopters and armoured vehicles moved into the mountainous region. The operation, which lasted several days, failed. Rumours circulated that there had been intelligence leaks which had allowed Karadžić to escape. It was the first time that NATO had publicly admitted carrying out an operation to arrest the former Bosnian Serb leader. It was to be the precursor for several more operations during the next six years.

As I sat at home looking over the rooftops of Sarajevo below, it became clear to me that if I wanted to pursue the Karadžić story, I would have to go to the town where the former Bosnian Serb President and his family had lived. The town of Pale, in the mountains not far from the capital, continued to be a hotbed of support for Karadžić . This was the place I needed to visit.

3

First Steps

'If this country cannot find the humanity to put aside its hate, it cannot have a future for its children' – Lord Ashdown, High Representative to Bosnia-Herzegovina, Inaugural Speech, 27 May 2002

The road winds out of Sarajevo, passing the Muslim cemetery on the right and the crumbling Turkish fort high up on a hill to the left. Down below, the old trade route to Istanbul, from the days of the Ottoman Empire, now no more than a gravel path, cuts its way through the valley. Just around here is the old frontline where Bosnian Government forces faced the Bosnian Serbs during the three-and-a-half-year siege. The road then climbs through a series of tunnels and emerges into a dramatic canyon where the mountains crowd in on either side. After the final tunnel, the road drops and the horizon widens into what could almost be a valley in the Swiss Alps. There are rolling green fields, patches of forest and a circular ring of mountains, giving the impression that you are in the middle of a huge bird's nest. At this time of year it was more beautiful than ever, covered in thick snow. In front of me was the town of Pale.

A few years earlier this was the beating heart of the Bosnian Serb war machine. It was the capital of Republika Srpska, seat of the Bosnian Serb Government and Presidency. It was where policy was made. It was also a place which did not see any fighting even though just a few miles away, in Sarajevo, sniping and shelling were the daily norm for everyone. In Pale, politicians and generals and would-be peacemakers engaged in endless rounds of negotiations to bring the slaughter to an end. Pale was the town to which Radovan Karadžić and his family had fled at the very start of the war, when the barricades went up in Sarajevo. Here he and his associates had held absolute sway.

It was winter and I was driving my dark blue 20-year-old Opel Kadett. I had bought it for 1,700 Bosnian Marks (about £600) from a friend in Sarajevo, but had never bothered to change the licence papers so as to avoid the extensive bureaucracy. I preferred driving this modest vehicle – not that I could afford anything more expensive – rather than the flashy, big-engined cars of the international community with their special gold and black number plates, all of which just reinforced their image of a distant and disconnected elite. As a journalist, blending in with the locals was a crucial part of being accepted.

Snow was falling again and the worn windscreen wiper was screeching across the glass. My eyes were concentrated on the road in front but my mind was wandering, trying to work out the best ways to follow up on my inquiries about the Karadžić case.

It was becoming apparent that, to make any real progress, I had to understand the Serb perspective. The Serbs had been vilified and attacked by everyone: the Muslims, the Croats, Western governments, NGOs, the UN, the EU, the OSCE. Not surprisingly, they had now hunkered down in their own communities, reluctant to speak to any outsiders. 'Everyone hates us so we will hate everyone else' seemed to be the unofficial motto. There was absolutely no trust in representatives of the Western media who were seen as partisan and as having contributed in large part to the 'propaganda war'. This image had been further bolstered by the recent conflict in Kosovo where, once again, the West had bombed the Serbs and the Western media had followed, spreading the anti-Serb message. And now the West and its allies were hunting down their former leaders and sending them to the War Crimes Tribunal at The Hague. There the vast majority of defendants were Serbs –

yet more proof, it was claimed, that they were victims of a grand conspiracy. The United States was regarded as the chief culprit but its allies, especially Britain, came a close second.

Other journalists who knew Bosnia and had covered the war had long since left the country, to chance their arm in new wars or to pursue alternative careers. Bosnia was rapidly sliding down the international news agenda and media houses were investing their resources elsewhere. Those journalists who did come to Bosnia stayed only for a few days, skimming the surface of a story, gathering a few sound bites and pictures, before jetting out again. I, on the other hand, was living in Bosnia, learning the language and had time on my side. I often regretted the fact that I had not been here during the bloody conflict, but the fact that I had not gave me a certain impartiality. I had no baggage which helped me achieve some credibility with the people I interviewed. They knew that I was not part of any bigger agenda. I also had the ability to listen, and if there is one thing that the people of the former Yugoslavia appreciate above all else, it is being listened to.

The snow had stopped falling as I left the last tunnel and began my descent into the open valley that is Pale. The official reason for my visit was to write a story about Karadžić's former colleague, a former university professor and third most senior politician in war-time Republika Srpska, Biljana Plavšić. The self-styled 'Serbian Iron Lady' of the Balkans, she had been a loyal ally of Karadžić during the war, adding a touch of brains and femininity to the Bosnian Serb leadership. In 1992, an infamous photograph had shown her stepping over the body of a dead Muslim civilian in order to kiss the notorious Serb warlord, Arkan. The incident had reinforced her credentials as a hard-line, uncompromising leader. In 2001, in a remarkable volte-face, she voluntarily handed herself in to the UN War Crimes Tribunal after learning that she had been indicted. She would eventually plead guilty to one count of 'crimes against humanity'. Her admission of guilt surprised many. It was the first time such a prominent Serb leader had shown even the slightest remorse. It shattered the wall of deniability that had been built up by the Bosnian Serbs over the years and was an important psychological breakthrough which would finally open up a debate, albeit a limited one, within the Serbian community itself about the rights and wrongs of the war they had fought.

I had come here to assess how Serbs now regarded one of their former leaders – as traitor or heroine? I wanted to speak not to the politicians and businessmen and police chiefs who made the headlines but to the workers, the mothers, the unemployed, the otherwise voiceless. The best place to do this would be at one of the many cafe-bars to be found throughout the Balkans. There are some clearly designed for a younger crowd, with shiny chairs, fake-marble floors and pumping music; and there are others which offer wooden chairs, a wood or concrete floor, and slightly slower, softer music.

The cafe I selected was full of old men, thick with smoke from their cheap cigarettes and pungent with alcohol fumes. As I walked in with my interpreter, Marko, chairs squeaked as a few of the customers twisted round to check out the unfamiliar faces. We sat down where some card-playing men in their fifties seemed to be finishing the dregs of their coffee. Marko told me that one of them used to work at the nearby Mercedes factory, but that had closed. Another was a maths teacher but earned only just enough to feed his family these days.

I introduced myself and tried to outline what I wanted. They just stared at me. One of them mumbled something. Another suddenly launched into a barrage of questions. Where are you from? How do we know you are really a journalist and not a spy? Why do you want to hear what we have to say now, when it is all too late? How do we know you'll report accurately what we say?

The door opened then, wafting in some welcome fresh air. Members of a wedding party that was taking place across the street stumbled in, laughing and joking. The men were wearing shiny suits with Serbian lapel badges. The women were in glorious shades of taffeta. All were smoking. I turned back to the table and made a few attempts to respond to the men's questions, but it was obvious that I was making no progress. Eventually we left the cafe and wandered down the street, glad to be out of the stifling atmosphere. We stopped a couple of women at random and I asked a few questions about Plavšić. 'She's a traitor,' was the terse reply.

My interpreter had arranged an interview with a former Bosnian Serb military commander. In a private room above his shop we sat down on fake black leather chairs and I requested his views on Plavšić. He listened intently as my interpreter translated. My grasp of the language was still not good enough for me to ascertain where he was going with his answer but he seemed passionate, animated, serious, sitting on the edge of his chair and leaning towards me to emphasise his points. The answer was interminable. It went along these lines: 'Well, we really must begin in 1389 . . .' To cut a very long story short, I was given a history of the Balkans dating back centuries, who was guilty of what and when, how this caused X to do that to Y, and then there was the Ottoman invasion, the fight for independence, the Second World War . . . You could not just view things in isolation, I was told. Everything was relative.

This was the pattern for so many other interviews I would conduct during my time in the former Yugoslavia. The long, 'historically based' response was usually a convoluted attempt to justify some particular crime of the recent past (and this would apply to all ethnic groups), and woe betide you if you tried to challenge this version of the truth. I cannot remember to this day what the ex-commander's views were on Plavšić, nor could my interpreter at the time. I am not even sure that the ex-commander himself knew what conclusion to draw.

Outside, a crowd had gathered in front of a building on the main street. Two big black cars with tinted windows came around the corner and pulled up. The crowd fell silent. The Prime Minister of Republika Srpska, Mladen Ivanic, climbed out, shook a few hands and was ushered inside. Marko warned me not to speak English out loud and we headed into the main hall, receiving pamphlets and smiles from the organisers. There were around 300 people present, including a surprising number of teenage girls. Did they have nothing better to do on a Saturday afternoon?

I surveyed peeling paint, wobbly chairs and benches, and tatty red curtains in front of the stage. The snow had turned to rain. You could hear it pitter-pattering on the roof. Stirring music suddenly blasted from the speakers. In unison, everyone sprang to their feet. It was the RS 'national' anthem. There followed a minute's silence for the Serb war dead, but nobody appeared to be counting and everyone was sitting down again within 30 seconds. A troop of politicians was hauled up on stage to bleat the well-worn lines. They were all introduced as 'Doctor', a typical technique used by politicians to imply academic credibility. One woman behind us exclaimed, 'They're all bloody doctors! Where am I going to find a doctor now if I need one?'

After the rally, I interviewed the Prime Minister outside under an umbrella. I subsequently learned he had studied for a while at Glasgow University which was why his English was so good. He told me nationalist issues were no longer so important. The economy was now key. He said he was prepared to work with the international community. Then he jumped into his car and was gone.

As we walked down the street, my interpreter suddenly prodded me and gave a nod of his head towards a man standing on the other side of the street. 'That man there . . . over there . . . he was Radovan's driver during the war,' he whispered. The man was well-built and sporting the black leather jacket and short hair that was almost de rigueur in these parts.

We crossed the street and my interpreter greeted him. The two of them exchanged a few smiles and pleasantries but I was pointedly not introduced. Clearly, my interpreter was of the opinion that introducing a British journalist was not going to win him any favours. I turned away and gazed irritably at a grey tower block across the street. My interpreter rejoined me and we began to move on when a car suddenly swung around the corner in front of us.

'That's Sonja, his daughter,' my interpreter said. 'Did you see?'

'Whose daughter, the driver's?'

'No! Radovan's. Sonja Karadžić.'

We left the centre of town and drove to the old Hotel Panorama overlooking the town. From there you could see the whole of Pale: the snow-covered roofs, the smoke rising from the chimneys, the sun trying to break through the cloudy sky. It looked beautiful; so peaceful, so pleasant, so innocent. The Hotel Panorama was the place where Karadžić had held many of his crucial Presidential meetings.

'You see the concrete pitch just down there?' said my interpreter, taking a drag of his cigarette. There was a pot-holed football pitch not far below us. 'They used to play football there during the war. They all used to take a break and come here to relax. One time, over a period of a few minutes, Radovan scored a goal, missed another easy chance and fouled somebody. I remember seeing what was shown on television that evening during the news reports. Each of the TV stations edited the version they wanted people to see. The Serbian channel showed him scoring a goal. The Croat TV channel showed him committing the foul. The internationals showed him missing the easy chance. Choose your truth.'

'And just behind us,' he continued, 'is where Radovan used to get his hair cut. The bodyguards would wait outside while Radovan used to go in. The barber had a good reputation.'

The drive back to Sarajevo did not take long. Another convoy of NATO troops, this time Italian Carabinieri, passed me, heading towards Pale. They were in a couple of jeeps and an armoured personnel carrier. The soldiers inside wore trendy black sunglasses. They were smiling and seemed to be enjoying the scenery. Were they going on another raid or was it just a regular patrol? Either way, they could be seen from far away by the people of Pale. Surprise was clearly no part of their agenda.

* * *

In the immediate aftermath of the Second World War, the authorities in the town of Šavnik provided materials for local people to begin rebuilding their communities. Petnica, three kilometres up the valley, was one of the villages to benefit. Families and friends, including the Karadžićs, worked together to repair each other's houses. Once one was complete, they'd move on to the next. Within a year, most of the village had been rebuilt.

Radovan Karadžić's parents, Vuk and Jovanka, had married during the war. Before that, Vuk Karadžić had worked as a farmer in Petnica. Jovanka moved from a nearby village in order to be with her husband. Radovan was the first of five children. He would eventually have three brothers – Luka, Ivan and Ratso – and one sister, Ivanka. During the war, Vuk had been a Četnik, fighting in and around the Šavnik area on the side of the royalists.

He had nearly paid the ultimate price for his loyalties. Relatives talk of an episode in 1944 when, during the night, a group of Partisans seized him from his home. They said they were taking him to headquarters but, either by design or on the spur of the moment, decided to execute him instead. According to the family, the group was passing through a wood when Vuk noticed that the Partisan guard in front of him had moved aside. He suspected this was a prelude to his being shot. He was right but, as the guards opened fire, Vuk threw himself on the ground. Although he was hit only slightly in the leg, he pretended to be dying and the Partisans, believing their job to be done, left the scene. When they had gone, Vuk shouted for help. Eventually his wife and sister-in-law came and rescued him. He walked with a limp for the rest of his life.

Radovan did not see much of his father in the years immediately after the war because Vuk was arrested and jailed in Podgorica. Relatives say it was because the victorious Partisans had been settling old scores from the war. Vuk had been accused of capturing a Partisan soldier and handing him over to the Četnik command. Subsequently, the prisoner had been executed. Whatever the truth of this, Radovan was five years old before he met his father. While in prison, Vuk trained as a cobbler. The skills he acquired would serve him well for the rest of his life. He had strong hands and a reputation for being able to turn his hand to most things. He also had a reputation as a very good guslar, a player and singer of the gusle, a one-stringed instrument similar to a violin, played by the southern Slavs.

The young Radovan was bright and well behaved. One villager remembers watching him playing for hours with some stones. He was less than two years old at the time. Jovanka was also watching him. Eventually they asked what he was doing. He said, 'I am trying to build a house.' The same villager remembers that Radovan never argued with other children: 'He was beautiful like an apple. He grew and developed well. He was very calm and quiet. And when he grew up he was very obedient, best of all of Vuk's children. I remember how well he developed, and how well his parents raised him. He was a good pupil, he learned well at school,'

He grew up in an environment of extreme hardship and uncertainty. The struggle against the invading Italians and Germans had been made more complicated and bloody by the concurrent civil war between Četniks and Partisans. Members of the same family fought on different sides, inflaming passions even more. The experience would be seared in the memories of all who survived it and would come back to haunt the next generation when war would once again break out in the region. Many would eventually justify their actions in the 1990s by referring to what had happened during World War II; some indeed would see the later war as a continuation of that one.

In November 1945 the new Yugoslav Constituent Assembly was formed. It formally abolished the monarchy, set up the Federal People's Republic of Yugoslavia and adopted the state's constitution. A year later, a Montenegrin Constituent Assembly adopted a new Montenegro Constitution and Montenegro became one of the six federal republics comprising Yugoslavia.

Some Četnik bands hid out in the woods and mountains of Montenegro for a couple of years after 1945 and there continued to be outbreaks of violence and revenge killings. But Tito's Partisans were now firmly in control of the government and the country. 'Bratstvo i Jedinstvo' (brotherhood and unity) was adopted as their new slogan. In an attempt to glue the shattered society back together, any form of nationalism was stamped out. At the same time, in order to allow things to move on and to avoid the never-ending witch hunt for World War II war criminals, a blind eye was turned to many crimes.

When Radovan was about six years old his father moved the family to the nearest big town, Nikšić, believing there would be more opportunities there. The government was gradually turning Nikšić into one of Montenegro's industrial centres. A steel mill was built in 1953 and the *population steadily expanded as people moved in from the surrounding countryside: from a post-war population of around 4,000 by the 1980s Nikšić had 50,000 inhabitants. Until the age of 15 this were where Radovan Karadžić lived and was educated. And then he would make the move that would change his life.*

In May 2002, the former leader of the British Liberal Democratic Party, Paddy Ashdown, arrived in Bosnia as the new chief international official to run the Office of the High Representative. His task was to oversee the implementation of the Dayton Peace Agreement. If he felt people were challenging or obstructing its implementation, he had wide-ranging powers to deal with the impasse including the ability to remove public officials and elected politicians from their jobs. Ashdown, a former Special Forces soldier of abundant energy, was not going to be shy of using these powers, either in his attempt to drag Bosnia out of its post-war political and economic mire or in his desire finally to resolve the war criminals issue.

He had experienced the Bosnian war at first hand, visiting Sarajevo during the siege and making frequent trips to the frontlines. He had been angered and moved by what he had seen. His was one of the few prominent international voices calling for Western intervention long before it arrived. He had developed a strong empathy for all the victims of the war and now felt it his duty to do what he could for the country. Not everyone would agree with his policies or his methods but Paddy Ashdown was a man quite prepared, if need be, to ruffle feathers in the pursuit of his objectives.

For months before his arrival, he had been preparing. He had taken Serbo-Croat lessons, courtesy of the British Foreign Office, and had selected a small team of high-flying British diplomats and personal assistants to mastermind an aggressive and fast-moving political and economic agenda which would be implemented as soon as he took up office. Several visits were made to Bosnia before his mandate would officially begin, in order to pave the way for the team's arrival. Links were established with politicians, journalists, and key players in the country. A team of eight British bodyguards was also assigned to oversee his personal security.

In the first few months after his arrival, Ashdown initiated a whole series of programmes, ranging from reforms within the court system, to anti-corruption measures, to a strategy for increasing employment. The policy went under the slogan: 'Jobs and justice through reform'. The pace was fierce, and by the time people had fully adjusted to one policy, he and his team had already moved on to the next. It was a dramatic departure from the more ponderous approach of previous High Representatives.

Ashdown wanted finally to make progress on the war crimes issue, and in particular to do all he could to force the arrest of the two individuals he saw as the chief architects of the Bosnian bloodbath: Ratko Mladić and Radovan Karadžić. He felt their continued freedom was on the one hand immoral and, on the other, a real obstacle to progress in the country. While these two men remained free, the Serbs would feel less of a compulsion to co-operate, and the Muslims and Croats would conclude there was too much unfinished business from the war for their full engagement in the reform process to be worthwhile.

Ashdown identified one key problem: the lack of co-ordination in the hunt for war criminals. As he put it: 'We were pursuing the policy of the lucky break: the intercepted phone call, the piece of intelligence which said he was here or there or there. We were depending on the avenging angel of justice in the form of an SFOR helicopter descending on a mountain forest glade and, in some dramatic coup de theatre, snatching him off to The Hague.'

He realised that this was always going to be a long shot. Karadžić was well protected, surrounded by loyal supporters, probably living in mountainous, remote territory where strangers and NATO vehicles could be identified long before they got anywhere near their target. Ashdown concluded that a more deliberate, methodical approach was called for. In

November 2002 he met SFOR commanders and senior Western intelligence officials in Bosnia to discuss a new strategy.

It was important to try and persuade the Serbs that Karadžić was not a hero, and that he should face justice for what he had done. They would make a concerted effort to tackle the alleged network of financial and logistical support that was protecting him. In practice this would mean targeting corrupt businessmen and politicians who were believed to be helping was crimes fugitives; freezing financial assets; introducing travel bans; carrying out raids on public and private properties and seizing evidence. Ashdown also lobbied the British Government hard to provide resources, especially Special Forces, to help in the hunt.

On 7 March 2003 Operation Balkan Vice was finally launched. In the first round of action, 14 individuals had their bank accounts frozen. One of these individuals was Karadžić himself. No one seemed to ask why it was only now that his bank account was being closed, eight years after he had been indicted by The Hague.

I had known Lord Ashdown vaguely during my time as a political reporter in Westminster when he had been leader of the Liberal Democratic Party. He had always appeared slightly aloof and his manner did not particularly endear him to colleagues or journalists. But in Bosnia he appeared to have changed.

On one occasion I wrote a story entitled 'A day in the life of Paddy Ashdown'. This entailed shadowing him as he left his Sarajevo home in the morning, then sitting in on a long list of meetings and engagements until his return home, a full twenty-four hours later. We walked to his office across the city with his bodyguards, unobtrusive in their jeans and rucksacks, following a few metres behind – a stark contrast to the flashing lights and monster vehicles the US Ambassador used to travel around in. We strode past the market-place where, during the war, Serb mortars had struck, killing dozens of civilians, one of the atrocities which had finally persuaded the West to take decisive action.

At work, Ashdown climbed the five flights of stairs to his office, leaving me, thirty years his junior, gasping for breath by the time I caught up. While he dealt with some more sensitive matters in his private office, I was left in a side room where some of his closest advisers were in the middle of an intense discussion. I listened as they debated the various legal and practical issues surrounding the creation of a Prime Minister for Bosnia. At that stage there was no one occupying that official role, there was only a 'Chairman of the Council of Ministers'. It was one of the central weaknesses of the state. Both the Muslim-Croat Federation and the Republika Srpska had their own Prime Ministers, but the state itself did not. The foreign advisers – there was not a Bosnian amongst them – were nonchalantly discussing the various legal and practical issues of creating this post without upsetting the parties within the two separate regions of Bosnia. It was a forceful example of the raw power and influence that OHR had over this nominally independent and democratic European state.

Later that morning we travelled by French military helicopter to the northern town of Bihać where Ashdown had a full programme. His wife Jane was accompanying us, and I was the only journalist taking the ride. As we crossed the mountains, with the rotor blades clattering, Ashdown closed his eyes for several minutes. It was not clear whether he was taking a short nap or simply reflecting upon bloodier times in Bosnia. He roused himself as the helicopter began to descend. A group of wild dogs ran for cover as we landed.

During the day Ashdown made a number of stops: from a small business that was offering rafting holidays; to a new border crossing where he would talk about the need for a single customs service across the country (to replace the two customs services currently being run by the Federation and the Republika Srpska); to a high school where he wanted to see for himself the facilities and conditions that pupils and teachers were having to deal with.

It was only in the evening that I got a real insight into an Ashdown I had never seen before. We were spending the night in a refugee transit centre in the small town of Bosanski Petrovac. The toilets were filthy, the urine covering your shoes as you paddled inside. A broken window provided a sort of ventilation in the form of an icy November wind. In one particularly drab room which served as a cafeteria, thick with smoke, Ashdown and his wife listened to the problems and tragic stories of a group of refugees, asking questions and trying to understand what these people had been through. He was taking notes which he would pass on to a colleague later, to see if anything could be done to help. Somehow these people had missed out on the aid that had been pumped into Bosnia by the international community. They were living in this centre because there was nowhere else for them to go, because their homes had been destroyed or occupied or they had no means to support themselves or . . . or . . . or . . . There were so many reasons.

Later I asked Ashdown why he had come to Bosanski Petrovac and what he thought he could really do here. 'This place, Bosnia, it got under my skin when I was here during the war. I have always taken an interest in its people. I have to do what I can,' he replied.

This was typical Ashdown. He would spend much of his nearly four years in Bosnia travelling to remote villages and towns, trying to connect with the 'real people', more often than not away from the scrutiny of cameramen and journalists. In his office he had a cartoon which summed up his views. It showed a row of tall, besuited men, probably Bosnian politicians, standing in front of a very small man. All the tall men are looking over their shoulders at the little man who is carrying a placard which reads 'Citizen'. Ashdown himself is portrayed standing in front of the suited men. He is saying, 'Excuse me, but it is that man that I am interested in.'

But despite the commitment of Bosnia's new High Representative, tracking down Karadžić was going to be far from easy. That became painfully obvious at the beginning of spring when SFOR peacekeepers raided a part of the building of the Republika Srpska (RS) Parliament which was believed to house an army intelligence unit. The unit was found to be intercepting international phone calls, targeting internationals, and running agents as far afield as NATO headquarters in Brussels.

At the end of February 2003 I made my first trip to Belgrade, to replace a colleague who was being sent to the Gulf as war threatened over Iraq. On the journey there I passed dozens of cars and coaches on the main Highway of Brotherhood and Unity, carrying supporters of the hard-line nationalist Serbian Radical Party. With their blue party flags streaming from the windows, they were travelling to the capital to say farewell to the party leader, Vojislav Šešelj. Their rabble-rousing figurehead was holding a final gathering before handing himself over to the UN War Crimes Tribunal in The Hague. My first job in the capital was to report on the rally.

Having dropped my bags off at the office, and after receiving a warning from my local colleagues to keep a low profile and not to speak English, I proceeded to Republic Square. There were around 8,000 people there, waving blue flags as well as more sinister black and white ones with a skull-and-crossbones motif. Some were drunk, some were wearing T-shirts bearing images of Karadžić or Mladić, and all were listening to the speeches from the stage outside the National Theatre where Šešelj and the party leadership were gathered. The whole event lasted no more than an hour but Šešelj gave his usual tub-thumping performance and declared that, although he would willingly travel to The Hague to prove his innocence, Karadžić and Mladić should never go. His supporters cheered and, at the end, set off on a march through the city centre. After a few more bottles of beer, they eventually drifted back to their cars and coaches. But I had felt their menace and anger, just as I had near Srebrenica.

No one knew it at the time, but Šešelj's farewell rally was just a prelude to an event three weeks later that would rock Serbia and threaten regional stability.

4

Assassination

"'I have to tell you, Serbia has lost everything today. We
now have our own J. F. Kennedy." She was pleading,
"Please don't let the West forget us. Please. Serbia is in
crisis. We are in crisis."' – Mourner at Zoran Djindjic's
funeral, 15 March 2003

Dirty grey clouds hung over the River Drina like some evil
portent as I walked across the broken, potholed bridge. On the
other side I could see the Serbian flag hanging limply by the
border post. Rain began to fall as I neared the barrier. Border
guards in waterproof jackets stood around, looking grim and
fingering the triggers of their Kalashnikovs. I had crossed at
this point several times before. Usually there were just two or
three guards milling around, looking bored and smoking. On a
good day you might even catch one of them smiling. But today
was different. Less than twenty-four hours earlier their Prime
Minister, Zoran Djindjic, had been assassinated. The perpetrators had escaped, a state of emergency had been declared, and
the country's security forces had been put on high alert.

I was the only pedestrian crossing the bridge and there were
fewer cars than usual making the trip. I could see the guards
suddenly become aware of my presence. They straightened up
and gripped their rifles. This was not going to be the usual
stamp in the passport and away you go. I finally reached the
barrier and walked up to the nearest guard. He looked down
at me with unblinking eyes.

I spoke in the limited Serbian I had learned, 'Hello.'

No answer, just an almost imperceptible movement of his head in my direction. Raindrops fell from his hat on to the gun barrel. His jaw clenched. I tried to offer him my passport but he indicated that I should wait for one of the other guards to come out of the blue Portakabin office.

'A bad day, isn't it?' I said, hoping he would understand that I was referring to the calamitous events in Belgrade. He just stared at me as if I was the last person on earth he wanted to talk to. Then he glanced away and focused on something else across the river. Another guard came out and took my passport without a word, disappearing back inside.

'Yes, it is a bad day,' the first guard said belatedly. 'It is raining.' Another long silence and then, as if a switch had been tripped in his mind, he relaxed. 'I guess it is like Ireland,' he said as if pleased to remember the name of the country.

'Yes, you're right . . . or even like Manchester,' I added.

'Ah . . . Manchester, yes!' His face brightened. 'Manchester United? You like Manchester United?'

If there were two words in the English language that were going to make you bond with someone in Bosnia, it was 'Manchester' and 'United'. It never ceased to amaze me how you could be travelling in the remotest village on the remotest Bosnian mountain – and virtually always see someone sporting the latest Manchester United shirt with 'Beckham' or 'Rooney' emblazoned on the back

I was near the border town of Zvornik, on my way from Bosnia to Serbia. The town had seen its fair share of horror and ethnic cleansing during the war. The non-Serbs had all been cleared out and were now living in other towns in Bosnia – or lying in the numerous mass graves which scarred the beautiful countryside. I was heading across the Drina on my way to Belgrade to report on the political convulsions occurring there. Although this was a major international news story, it was struggling to make headlines in the West because of recent events in the Middle East.

The second guard reappeared and beckoned for me to follow him into the blue Portakabin. As we walked inside, I noticed a calendar hanging from the wall which displayed two large photographs of Ratko Mladić and Radovan Karadžić.

I was ushered along a corridor and then into a small smoke-filled room. At his desk, an official was waiting to question me.

'Who are you? What do you want?' he snapped.

'I'm a journalist, travelling to Belgrade to report on the assassination of your Prime Minister. Is there a problem?' He looked down at my passport, then up at my face.

'How do I know that you are not a member of Al-Qaeda?'

'I'm sorry?'

'How do I know that you are not a member of Al-Qaeda?'

I thought he was joking and began to smile. But a second glance at his face told me he was being absolutely serious.

'I am not a member of Al-Qaeda. I am a British journalist. It says so in my documents.' I pointed to the press pass he was holding in his hands. I was about to say something more then bit my tongue. Across the room two of his colleagues sat in silence, one reading a newspaper, the other playing with his pistol.

The commander suddenly started to smile.

'Rodney and Del Boy, eh?' he said, nodding in the direction of the other two guards.

'What?'

His smile broadened and gradually I realised he was refer-ring to the famous British comedy series *Only Fools And Horses*. It was the last thing on earth that I was expecting, but I guess I had the BBC's foreign rights department to thank for selling the series to Serbia and thereby giving me a way out of a potentially nasty situation.

'Those two, they are Del Boy . . . and Rodney.' He started to laugh when he realised I understood. 'And maybe you . . . you . . .' he could hardly contain his laughter '. . . you could be Granddad!'

He laughed heartily at his own joke. Suddenly he produced his mobile phone and pointed to a picture of Red Star Belgrade football team on the screen. He kissed it extravagantly and switched to speaking English. 'Me, I luv best football team Red Star Bellgred!'

A few minutes later my passport had been stamped, I had found a taxi and was on my way to Belgrade.

A single sniper's bullet had ended the life of Serbia's Prime Minister, Zoran Djindjic. The previous day he had arrived at his office in the centre of Belgrade and got out of his car. It had just gone midday. He was hobbling on crutches because of a football injury. The bullet was fired from a point less than 200 metres away. The sniper was positioned in a semi-derelict yellow-painted building on the far side of a small park.

The window he'd chosen had a perfect view over the car park; it was an easy shot for an experienced sniper. The wounded Djindjic was quickly bundled into a car by his bodyguards and they screeched off, lights flashing, to hospital. But it was too late. A state of emergency was declared, special police units were deployed on the streets of the capital, and border security was stepped up.

Zoran Djindjic had been one of the key figures in Serbia uniting opposition to the autocratic and disastrous rule of President Slobodan Milošević, who had eventually been overthrown by a popular and bloodless revolt in October 2000. Subsequently, Djindjic had become Prime Minister, advocating pro-Western policies, massive reform and co-operation with the UN War Crimes Tribunal in The Hague. But the temporary alliance that had overthrown Milošević soon splintered, amidst bitter recriminations, into different factions. The main split occurred between Djindjic and the future Prime Minister and nationalist politician, Vojislav Koštunica. Djindjic's personal popularity declined as he began to challenge various power structures within the country and he came under increasing attack.

Crucially, he also lent his support for the transfer of Milošević to The Hague. He was keen to introduce reform to Serbia and, at the same time, improve the country's image abroad after the isolation of the 1990s. But it was a dangerous tactic. Organised crime, corruption and extreme nationalist forces had their own interests to protect. After Milošević was packed off to The Hague, they feared they could be next. So the assassination did not come as a complete surprise. But the fact that it had happened with such apparent ease, in broad daylight and in the very heart of Belgrade, actually outside the Prime Minister's office, was a clear indication of the power and confidence of those darker forces within Serbian society. It was less than two years since Milošević had been overthrown. The country had begun to move on from the wars and sanctions of the 1990s. The fractious government might have been making slow progress, but, at least that process had been democratic. Djindjic had been beginning to build bridges with the outside world. All he had achieved was now in jeopardy.

It was a long drive to the capital along a single, poorly surfaced road. There was little to indicate the current political turmoil, except for the Serbian flags hanging at half mast outside petrol stations and the increased number of police patrols. In villages, the ancient blue and white Zastava police cars, which looked like oversized wheelbarrows with roofs attached, loitered at junctions. But things were very different in the capital. Police officers were stationed at every major road intersection; random checks were being carried out on cars and passengers. I travelled down the main road, Kneza Miloša, where the government ministries and foreign embassies were situated. Outside all the main buildings, units of the paramilitary Gendarmerie were stationed. These special police wore green camouflage uniforms and face masks. They were carrying assault rifles and looked ready to use them. You could feel the tension.

At the entrance to the street where Djindjic had been shot, men in black leather jackets were speaking into walkie-talkies. Black Audis came and went. More special police in green bulletproof jackets and carrying Kalashnikovs eyed me as I stood watching the scene. Women carrying flowers, and with tears in their eyes, walked past.

Another unit of Gendarmerie was stationed outside the main

door. Round the corner was a queue of people, several hundred strong. They had come to sign a book of condolence. More tears and flowers. Some were carrying candles and photographs of the former Prime Minister. There was absolute silence apart from the sounds of the passing traffic. In front of the main doors, a pile of wreaths and cards was mounting. Candles were burning amidst the flowers. In one corner the flames from a dozen candles merged into one. I watched as the orange wax ran down the pavement and froze into a huge pool close to the gutter.

I went to the place from where the assassins had struck. Outside the empty office building with crumbling paintwork, three dogs were stretched out enjoying the sun's feeble rays. Next to the building was a restaurant. Witnesses claimed they'd seen three men in dark blue overalls leave the offices immediately after the shooting. Armed police were now directing people away from the little park between the sniper's vantage point and the place where Djindjic had fallen.

In the afternoon, I crossed the river to Zemun where it was believed the perpetrators of the crime were based. More units of the Gendarmerie had taken up position outside a four-storey modern building which was bristling with security cameras and lights. Word on the street was that this place was owned by one of those involved in the assassination. Bulldozers had been brought in. A crowd had gathered to watch, among them a number of journalists. The scene was being broadcast live on national television. The bulldozers moved in and a cheer went up. The authorities were trying to make a point.

Three days later, the demolition was still ongoing and still on television, in case anyone doubted their determination.

Zoran Djindjic's funeral took place on a bright, sunny day. The temperature hovered above freezing as Belgrade came to a stand-still and half a million people thronged the streets. Djindjic's coffin lay draped in a Serbian flag in the great-domed Cathedral of Saint Sava. Mourners streamed past, paying their last respects.

Loudspeakers relayed the service to the thousands gathered

in the park outside, carrying pictures and candles, unable to get in. I stood in the mud with them. There was a look almost of bewilderment on many of the faces around me.

When the service was over, I watched as the crowd snaked its way through the city centre towards the cemetery where the former Prime Minister would be laid to rest. There was only the sound of dragging footsteps and a single helicopter circling above.

A blonde woman in her twenties approached me, tears in her eyes.

'Are you a journalist? Where are you from?'

'Yes, from Britain.'

'I have to tell you,' she said between sobs, 'Serbia has lost everything today. We now have our own J. F. Kennedy.' She looked at me, almost beseechingly. 'Please don't let the West forget us. Please. Serbia is in crisis. We are in crisis.'

Moments later a man approached me and, realising I was foreign, told me he wanted to say something into my microphone. 'When Tito died,' he said, 'people came out on to the streets because they felt they had to. But today people have come out because they want to. That is the difference.'

In the evenings, the television schedules were dominated by coverage of the assassination and the funeral. The news was usually followed by a conspiracy feature film like *JFK*, *The Godfather* or *Patriot Games*, tapping into the mood of the nation.

Some 500,000 Serbs, one in sixteen of the entire population, had attended Zoran Djindjic's funeral. They knew what they had lost and did not want to return to the dark old days. They were only too aware that, waiting in the wings, were the hard-line nationalists with their links to organised crime, who would happily assume power once again and try to turn back the clock. Only later did I discover that the murder had taken place on the birthday of Ratko Mladić.

The assassination of the Prime Minister revealed the fragility of Serbia's newfound democracy. It remained to be seen who was responsible and whether it was part of some wider plan to change the government. In a massive police operation, codenamed Operation Sabre, 10,000 people would be arrested across Serbia. Well-known criminals, politicians, members of the judiciary, even pop stars, were taken into custody. Even the former President Vojislav Koštunica's chief security adviser and future head of the intelligence service, Rade Bulatović, was detained for a time. Checkpoints were set up around major cities such as Novi Sad and Niš, and, for the first time, police were deliberately stopping big, expensive cars with tinted windows, the ones they had always avoided in the past. They were specifically on the look-out for members of a criminal gang which had been accused of involvement in the murder. The television news regularly showed film of big men with bull necks and crewcuts, being handcuffed and shoved into waiting police vans.

As time passed, rumours began to circulate about an elite police unit known as the Red Berets. The unit had been formed under Milošević in 1991. Some of its members had participated in the Bosnian War and, it was alleged, had had close links to the notorious Serbian paramilitary group known as Arkan's Tigers, which was accused of carrying out some of the worst atrocities of the war. The Red Berets had originally been loyal to Milošević but, when they detected a change in the wind in October 2000, had refused to intervene on their leader's behalf, which ultimately helped the democratic opposition to assume the reins of power. The Red Berets had thrown in their lot with the new government. They might even have been involved in Milošević's arrest and eventual transfer to The Hague. But their good relations with the new regime had deteriorated as Djindjic made plans to tackle organised crime and co-operate with the Hague Tribunal. The Red Berets held a street protest against this in the centre of Belgrade. And then the authorities named a former head of the unit, an ex-French Foreign Legionnaire, Milorad Ulemek Luković (also known as Legija), as the chief suspect in Djindjic's murder. There were suggestions that the unit would now be disbanded.

The Red Berets' base was in the small town of Kula, close

to the border with Croatia, a 45-minute drive from Belgrade. There were no signposts. After a number of confused directions from locals, I drove up a lane past the local cemetery. The road dipped and came to an abrupt end. Straight ahead was the Red Berets' base. There was a Stop sign and a notice forbidding photography. A single guard stood to attention in the road ahead. Through a line of trees behind the fence, I could make out what looked like some new buildings and a small air traffic control tower. It had been rumoured that units loyal to the government were encircling the area, but there was no sign of any activity. This had obviously been a wasted journey.

I took the main highway back to Belgrade. All of a sudden, four Serbian military helicopters came into view, flying in formation. Two minutes later, five military jets soared overhead. Something was going on but I had no idea what.

I had the feeling that Serbia was poised on the brink of collapse. The state was under threat and did not know how to respond. Who was now in charge? Who was actually running the country? As we neared the capital, the police patrols were even more conspicuous. You could feel the tension in the air. Serbia was in crisis. But in less than a week, whatever was going on there became of minor interest to news editors in London and beyond: American cruise missiles were launched against Baghdad.

In 1960 15-year-old Radovan Karadžić finished elementary school in Nikšić. He left the mountains of north-west Montenegro and made his way to the Bosnian capital, Sarajevo.

Sarajevo was the third most important city of Yugoslavia after Belgrade and Zagreb. Now, with the hardships of the war years receding, money was beginning to flow into the city, industry was growing, and new housing was being created to cater for the influx of migrants from the country, eager to better their lot.

Radovan enrolled in junior medical school. He earned money by delivering milk and newspapers, sending some of the cash back to his family in Montenegro. Not long after arriving in Sarajevo, he joined the Communist Party – the obvious thing to do for an ambitious young student when any advancement in Socialist Yugoslavia was dependent on member-ship of the ruling party. In 1964 he moved on to study medicine at Sarajevo University. There were 180 students in his year but one in particular caught his eye soon after the course began. Her name was Ljiljana Zelen and she would eventually become his wife.

In sixties Sarajevo the Beatles and Tom Jones were all the rage. Students would go dancing at Sloga, a club that still exists today. There was no coffee-shop society for the young and impoverished, as there is now. Instead, most students spent their spare time engaged in the corso: *meandering up and down the city's main street. The young people tended to keep to the side where the Kafana Park was located, the older people to the other. In those days it did not matter whether you were Muslim, Serb or Croat.*

Radovan was tall and thin, almost gangly, with hair worn longer than most of his peers'. He dressed in a Bohemian way, and was regarded as something of an outsider. He lived in student accommodation in the Bjelave area, not far from the centre and with a view of the city below. He worked as a part-time sanitary inspector to earn extra money. But he spent most of his time with his girlfriend, Ljiljana. The two were inseparable – studying together, eating together, and walking together during the evening corso. *By this time he had already begun writing poetry. One contemporary remembers chatting to Radovan between classes at university, and the young man from Montenegro saying he was only studying medicine as a hobby. He did not know what else to do.*

On 28 March 1967 Radovan and Ljiljana were married. The wedding took place in Bačka Topola, near Subotica in northern Serbia, where Ljiljana's cousin lived. There were only around a dozen guests. There was no honeymoon, which was not unusual at the time for relatively poor students. Their daughter, Sonja, was born soon after.

As student demonstrations swept Europe in 1968, Yugoslavia was not immune. Sarajevo saw its own student demonstrations in the spring and Radovan Karadžić played his part. The main protest took place outside the Government Building where today's Presidency is located. Like other young people across Yugoslavia, the students wanted better accommoda-tion and more financial support. There was some violence and windows in the Kafana Park buildings were smashed. The police gave as good as they got. According to some, Radovan made an emotional nationalist speech from the roof of the Faculty of Philosophy in Sarajevo, after which, the family claims, he was placed under constant surveillance by Yugoslav secret police.

After the demonstrations, he was also thrown out of the Communist Party. The excuse given was an article he had written, but his involvement in the demonstrations was almost certainly the real reason according to his wife, who claims it was from that moment on that life became more difficult for him and his family. There were allegations that he eventually became a police informant, something strongly denied by everyone close to him. The family says that it was around this time that the sense of 'being an outsider', someone who was not part of the system or even a dissident, began to form in his mind.

He had already been writing for some time. He produced his own pamphlet called Ponocnik which included both poems and stories he had written. He was also writing articles and poems for several magazines and newspapers and had some work broadcast on a local radio station. His first book was published in 1968. Finally, after seven years of study, he received his medical degree from the University of Sarajevo on 19 July 1971.

A short time after the murder of Djindjic I arranged to go to Romania with a colleague from another news agency, to report on the country's efforts to join the European Union. On the last day, my colleague received a strange phone message from Belgrade. The caller would only identify himself as someone working for the Serbian police but said he was very keen to talk to my colleague once he returned. No other information was given. Operation Sabre was still in full swing and my colleague became concerned that the general round-up of people, currently numbered in the thousands, could now be targeting the media. Might he be arrested for some non-crime? Anything seemed possible in the paranoia currently engulfing Serbia.

But when we arrived at Belgrade airport there was no police van waiting for us. Later in the week, my colleague was called again and invited for a coffee in a downtown Belgrade bar. Afterwards he told me that it had been an attempt by the Serbian security service to recruit him. He was asked to report regularly on my work, told this would be a patriotic service for Serbia. In return, he was offered help with a business he was trying to start. Foreign journalists had been targeted since the Milošević era. It was generally accepted these days that our phones would be monitored and our movements observed by the security services. My colleague showed considerable bravery in declining the offer, but they did not give up easily. He would receive further invitations.

Meanwhile, the authorities were making progress towards uncovering the assassination conspiracy. Apparently, the Prime Minister had been only the first on a list of people destined to be eliminated. The ultimate aim was to destabilise the country and enable the return to power of former allies of Milošević. But no more murders took place and a group of suspects was identified and taken into custody.

I was granted an interview with Serbia's new Defence Minister, and future President, Boris Tadić. Born in Sarajevo, he was young and relatively inexperienced but he had been a close friend of Djindjic and had shared the latter's desire not only to see the country embrace reform, but to move closer to joining international organisations such as the European Union. The interview took place in the Defence Ministry building, a few hundred metres from where the assassination had taken place. Part of it was still in ruins from the NATO bombing of Belgrade during the Kosovo conflict of 1999, a potent reminder, as some saw it, of Western antipathy to the Serbs.

As I waited in reception, a man dressed in civilian clothes came in and sat next to me. In a casual manner, he started asking me questions about who I was, how long had I been in Serbia and what exactly I was doing in the country. I asked who he was and he gave me some long convoluted title which left me none the wiser. He asked a few more questions and said that he had once worked in the United Kingdom, though under what circumstances was far from clear. Eventually he got up and left. A couple of minutes later, a man in military uniform came in and said the Defence Minister would now see me.

Tadić's office, high up in the building, was sparsely furnished, the chairs and sofas made of black faux-leather. There were a few modern paintings on the wall. A Yugoslav flag hung behind his desk, next to a picture of Djindjic. Throughout the interview Tadić spoke without the presence of advisers or press officials, unusual for such an important politician. He told me about his friendship with Djindjic, and explained how his life had changed recently with all the protective measures now surrounding him.

I pointed out to him that the Serbian Government like himself seemed relatively young and inexperienced. He asked me whether I thought that was a good or bad thing. I had no reply. I asked him who was giving him advice during these difficult times. He said, no one. Later, he told me the Serbian military was in need of reform. I asked him about relations with The Hague, and about Karadžić and Mladić. He said he could not rule out the possibility that Mladić, as a former soldier, might be receiving protection from elements within the Serbian military. In a candid moment he admitted that he could not say that he had 100 per cent control over his own armed forces. He seemed isolated. But, then again, so did Serbia.

In January 2003 another raid by SFOR peacekeepers had targeted the Sveti Jovan radio station in Pale, owned and controlled by the wife and daughter of Karadžić. In the same month, the new US Ambassador for War Crimes, Pierre-Richard Prosper, arrived in Bosnia and directly threatened the Bosnian Serb Republic with sanctions if they did not start to co-operate over the Karadžić issue. I secured an interview with him at which he said progress was being made. He also revealed that the US Rewards for Justice programme, which was offering $5 million for information leading to the arrest of Karadžić or Mladić, had recently paid out $250,000 to an individual in the region.

'I agree that too much time has passed on the question of Karadžić,' Prosper told me. 'But we're prepared to wait as long as it takes to bring him into custody. We are prepared to provide information. We have provided information. We have given the authorities in the region an opportunity to take action, which has not happened. They too have an active responsibility.' Prosper promised more was to come. 'There are people of influence who form part of his network. We plan to approach these persons in due course,' he added.

Prosper met Lord Ashdown and, afterwards, the British diplomat declared that they would now 'formulate measures to begin to take action against those who support the structures which are supporting Karadžić'. He would not be more precise simply adding, 'If you can imagine it, we are thinking of it.'

In April, the European Union introduced a travel ban on certain individuals who were 'engaged in activities helping persons at large to evade justice for crimes of which the International Criminal Tribunal for The Hague has indicted them'. In July, the list of these individuals was extended to include members of the Karadžić family, former associates of theirs, businessmen and senior politicians. A Serbian Orthodox Bishop was officially banned from travelling to the European Union for supporting Karadžić, only for it to be realised later that the cleric had died several years before. The assets of some of these people were also frozen. In August, the pressure was stepped up with a raid on the house of Ratko Mladić's mother who had died the previous night. At the beginning of September, for the first time, Bosnian Serb police carried out an operation, raiding the home of the Orthodox Serb Bishop Vasilije Kačavenda in the north-eastern town of Bijeljina.

As the effort against the support network increased, I found myself back in Belgrade for a long-awaited meeting with one of Karadžić's closest supporters. Outside the Hotel Moscow in the centre of Belgrade I sat sipping bitter lemon juice. The sun was out and the parasols were open but it felt cold nevertheless. The person I was meeting was late but I thought his curiosity would get the better of him and I was not wrong. Kosta Čavoški, small and businesslike, appeared from nowhere and took a seat opposite me. One of Karadžić's strongest supporters, the one-time law professor, one-time senior politician in Karadžić's Republika Srpska, writer and staunch defender of his former leader, examined me with interest. He told me he was editing a new book related to Karadžić's correspondence during the war, but did not know when it would be published. After that introduction our conversation was short.

'Do you know where he is?'

'No.'

'Do you know how I could contact him?'

'No.'

'Could you get a message to him?'

'No.'

'Is he in Bosnia?'

'I don't know.'

'Is he here in Belgrade, in Serbia?'

'I don't know.'

Of course, Čavoški would almost certainly not tell me anything even if he did have inside knowledge. His code of loyalty was just too strong. I realised then that this interviewing approach to finding information was going to prove extremely difficult. So I decided that, while I would continue to pursue such lines of enquiry whenever possible, there were more practical steps I could take. For instance, it had been rumoured for some time – again with no hard evidence – that the mountainous area of south-east Bosnia was the most likely place for Karadžić to hide. It was high time I visited it myself. At just the right moment the opportunity arose for me to make the trip – in the company of Bosnia's chief international official.

In the heat of the Bosnian summer, we made the trip south towards the border with Montenegro. Snakes slithered across the road ahead of our car; others lay squashed on the steaming tarmac behind us. This barren land resembled a moonscape with its cratered white rock; only the stubby, gnarled bushes were a reminder that we were not on another planet. The heat was stifling, aggravated by the fact that we had no air conditioning in our vehicle. This was Herzegovina, an area of country famous for its hard terrain and harder people.

We were heading towards the southern town of Trebinje, not far from the border with Montenegro. I was accompanying Lord Ashdown who wanted to show his support for the newly founded State Border Service (SBS) whose job it was to patrol the border of Bosnia-Herzegovina. During the next two days Ashdown visited a number of border posts and spoke to officials there, gaining first-hand knowledge of the problems of trying to monitor such a porous border, with its mountainous landscape and numerous hidden paths.

The trip had its farcical side. An SBS patrol boat broke down in the middle of a huge lake which was known to be a smugglers' haunt. Ashdown had intended to join a dawn raid there with the officers but their boat was left drifting uselessly. An alternative plan was hastily conjured up by his advisers and we set off for our other appointments.

On the way back, Ashdown wanted to travel on public transport so as to get an idea of what it was like. At a bus station bar in Bileća, a hard-line Serb town, he engaged in conversation with a couple of locals. A photographer, travelling with our party, spotted an opportunity and moved quickly around the bar, crouching below Ashdown's eyeline. The next day the biggest-selling newspaper in the country, the pro-Muslim *Dnevni Avaz*, displayed the picture on its front page: Ashdown was shown leaning on the bar. Behind him on the wall, for all to see, was a picture of Radovan Karadžić.

The caption to the photograph read: 'At a time when SFOR and the whole Western world have been searching for the most wanted war crimes indictee, the High Representative of the same international community held official talks under a picture of Radovan Karadžić posted on the wall. We will see if this incredible scandal is a good enough reason for Ashdown to do the honourable thing and resign from his post.'

The honeymoon period was over. From that day on, Ashdown would not be judged by his rhetoric. He would be judged on whether his actions would lead to the arrest of war criminals, especially Radovan Karadžić.

5

Funerals

'I'll always feel his arms around me. He put his hands
over his eyes and said, "Mummy, I don't want to see you
leaving." I was looking back for a long time and I could
see he was still holding his hands over his eyes. I have
that picture in my head all the time and it will never
disappear. Never' – Hatidza Mehmedovic, President of
the Association of the Mothers of Srebrenica

It was the season for funerals. Under a baking hot sun, the
widows stood or sat, listening to the words of Bill Clinton.
The coffins of their menfolk, covered in green canvas, lay on
the dry mud next to the open graves. The women listened in
sombre silence, their minds elsewhere, their hands clutching
water bottles or the person closest to them. There was the
occasional wail or scream when everything became too much
but, in truth, their silent dignity was impressive. It was
September 2003.

Here, in this valley, eight years previously, life as they had
known it had stopped for them. They had been separated
from their loved ones for the last time. Lines of buses had
transported the women across the frontlines to safety while
the men and boys were taken away. The subsequent massacre
took place over the period of a week. The captives were herded
into buildings or lined up alongside trenches, before being
machine-gunned, burned or stabbed to death. It would be a
while before the world learned the fate of these people. By

the time the horrific story emerged, their killers had dug up many of the bodies from the mass graves and reburied them elsewhere, in an attempt to conceal the crime. In the process, the remains became entangled, broken or divided – victims inextricably mingled in death.

I saw my first mass grave in a beautiful village by a river not far from Srebrenica. I remember hearing birdsong in the trees as I approached. Pathologists were scraping mud from bones. They did it in silence, working methodically. There were just so many bones. The grave itself resembled some kind of rubbish tip, like the ones you find on waste ground at the edge of cities – a jumble of clothes, household goods and mud. It was always impossible to say how many corpses had been dumped in a particular grave. If you find a thigh bone and make a DNA match with three teeth in the same grave, does that mean you have found a body?

Srebrenica itself was now in Republika Srpska, a trophy of war. Very few Muslims returned there after the war ended, fearing for their lives or simply tortured by their memories. One of those who did come back was Abdullah, the irrepressibly cheerful owner of the best restaurant in town. Before the war, he had been the cookery teacher at the local high school. During the war he had worked for Médecins Sans Frontières in the town. When he tells you the stories, his face clouds over and, for once, his cheerfulness is muted. He saw a lot but says little. His work with the French aid agency secured him a ticket out of the place when the Serbs moved in. After the war, when things had quietened down, he returned to the town and opened the restaurant where he acts as owner, chef and waiter. 'It's my town as much as anybody else's,' he told me.

But Muslims would come back in large numbers whenever there was a burial in the new cemetery, like today. One of the blackest ironies of this particular day was that most of the security for the event was being provided by the Bosnian Serb police, some of whom, it was alleged, were involved either directly or indirectly in the massacre itself. But the presence of

SFOR troops and so many international VIPs provided the assurance of security needed for the Muslims to return, at least for a day.

Clinton, no longer President of the United States, had come to open formally the memorial cemetery for the thousands of men and boys who had been killed. I stood a few metres away, listening to his words spoken in that customary slow, thoughtful drawl.

> We remember this terrible crime for we dare not forget, because we must pay tribute to the innocent lives, many of them children, which were snuffed out in what must be called genocidal madness. Srebrenica laid bare for all the world to see the vulnerability of ordinary people to the dark claims of religious and ethnic superiority. Bad people who lusted for power killed these good people simply because of who they were. They sought power through genocide. Those most responsible for the atrocities, the leaders, have not been apprehended. The search for them must continue until they are. We owe it to the men and boys buried in this hallowed ground, we owe it to the wives and children who survived them, and we owe it to all Bosnian children yet unborn to see that justice is done.

The small, cheap coffins were lowered into the earth. They were very light, most containing no more than a few teeth and bones, perhaps the odd skull. No one wanted to tell the relatives that the contents were so pitiful. There came the sudden rhythmic thud of soil being shovelled on to a thousand coffins. There were wailing cries and glances turned to the heavens. At least the dead had now found their final resting place.

One of the rumours that had been circulating for some time was that Karadžić had struck a deal with Clinton or his associates at the end of the war. The allegation was that Karadžić was offered immunity from prosecution at The Hague if, in return, he resigned his political posts and withdrew into private life. I wanted to put this to Clinton himself, but all the journalists had been told that the former President would be giving no interviews. He would just make his speech and then leave.

As the other VIPs left the cemetery, Clinton, surrounded by nervous and sweating bodyguards, decided to wander among the graves. He was accompanied by the head of the Islamic community in Bosnia and the Muslim President. I thought an English voice in a crowd of Bosnian widows might attract his attention and thrust my hand out in the hope he would shake it. He did. I did not let go but looked him in the eye.

'Mr Clinton,' I said, 'why hasn't Karadžić been caught?' He stood still. His bodyguards seemed momentarily nonplussed. Out of the corner of my eye, I could see them close in.

'I've been surprised they haven't gotten him . . .' Clinton's next words were lost in the noise of the crowd around us.

'You didn't do a deal with him in 1995, to say that if you disappear . . .'

'No . . . absolutely not.'

'Because there are all sorts of rumours in this country . . .'

'I know that. But I can tell you, in the beginning when we took over, we, the American forces, were in charge of the area where we thought he was. So I did my best. I can tell you . . .' Again his words were lost in the noise from the crowd.

'You see, there are lots of conspiracy theories here that America did do a deal and that is why Karadžić is still free.'

'Yes, I know that . . . but I can assure you, no deal was done. I would never have done that. This man needs to face justice for what he did.' There was a pause and I tried frantically to think of a follow-up question. But I was too late. The body-guards, increasingly concerned about the situation, gently but forcefully moved Clinton along. He turned away and continued down the path, shaking hands and listening to words he did not understand. A few seconds later he disappeared amidst the widows.

As I walked back to the entrance to the cemetery, Clinton's

helicopter lifted into the air, the clattering rotor blades sending a veil of dust over the freshly dug graves.

A German colleague, Markus Bickel, who had travelled with me to the funeral and was also pursuing the Karadžić story, suggested we cross the road to the huge, derelict building opposite. This was the old battery factory which eight years previously, as Srebrenica descended into hell, became the final outpost of the out-gunned, out-manoeuvred UN Dutch battalion which had been the last line of defence against Ratko Mladić's Bosnian Serb forces. The factory had been the only refuge for thousands of Muslim civilians as the Serbs took control of the town and surrounding area.

Film footage shows Ratko Mladić strutting around the perimeter fence offering words of reassurance and sympathy to the terrified civilians inside. But when the cameras turned away, as witnesses later testified, some of those inside the compound were dragged off by Serb soldiers and killed in nearby fields.

I once interviewed one of the Dutch soldiers who was in the compound at the time. With tears in his eyes he described the scene: 'It was mayhem. I saw the whole of humanity here. I saw old people dying, babies being born, people hanging themselves, people crying. It was hell. I never want to see that again.'

There had been talk of turning the derelict building into a museum, but there were no visible signs of that happening. We entered the cavernous hall, our footsteps echoing on the dusty floor. Twisted metal and crumbling brickwork encircled a hole left by a tank shell. We wandered around the corridors and abandoned rooms, broken glass crunching under our feet. The sun was setting over the nearby hills and its rays bathed us in a warmth neither of us felt.

We separated, lost in our own thoughts, exploring different rooms. Suddenly Markus shouted out to me. I found him staring at some graffiti on a wall. As I scanned the writing, it became clear that this was not the recent work of vandals, but had been written by some of the UN troops stationed in Srebrenica during the war, not just the Dutch but soldiers of other nationalities too. Some of the scribble was harmless, the sexual imagery perhaps to be expected, but other words were simply shocking:

No teeth?
A moustache?
Smell like shit?
Bosnian girl!

My ass is like a local –
it's got the same smell!

Bosnia '94

We walked back downstairs into the huge hangar-like hall. Now we were looking for any other graffiti we might have missed the first time round. In a dark alcove, at just about head-height, we found some more, barely legible, words. This time they were not obscenities written by soldiers but perhaps the last words of someone hemmed in with nowhere left to go:

Greetings to Rizo and Sahid and everyone. I am forgotten.

On another visit to Srebrenica, I sat on a bench in the memorial cemetery while black storm clouds gathered overhead. Hatzida, a widow, was telling me how she had lost her husband and two sons in July 1995:

When I sleep, I dream about the last time I saw them, and when I dream about it, I wish I will never wake up. I can hear now the words of my youngest son, saying, 'Mummy don't come with us. Go to the United Nations base. You'll get tired otherwise.' And he was hugging me and I'll always feel his arms around me. And when the time came to part, he put his hands over his eyes and said, 'Mummy, I don't want to see you leaving.' I was looking back for a long time and I could see he was still holding his hands over his eyes. I have that picture in my head all the time and it will never disappear. Never.

To that day, Hatzida did not know where they were. She had returned to live in Srebrenica two years previously, braving the threat from the Serbs who now dominated the town. She showed me photographs of her family. She said the only truth for her would come when 'I know who killed my sons, who ordered it, who buried them, and who drove the digger machine over the grave'. As we walked out of the deserted cemetery, lightning cracked overhead and the heavens opened.

Another time, another visit to Srebrenica, another widow. There was a puddle at the bottom of the lane where she lived. Some little birds were splashing there to cool their wings. The rain had gone and the sun was bursting through. The woman was planting vegetables in her garden when we arrived. There were no men left in her family. As she tilled the soil, she told us that when she had returned to her house after the war, she had found a human head in the garden. She did not know to whom it had belonged. She said it all so casually, not missing a stroke of her tilling.

In a village on the outskirts of Srebrenica, a Serb man was sitting next to his homemade distillery by the stream. He invited us to join him in a glass of his freshly made *rakia* or plum brandy. He told me how the Serbs had been overrun in an attack by Muslims from Srebrenica on Christmas Day, 1993. He said some of his comrades were killed and mutilated: 107 Serbs lost their lives. He was not sure why so many Muslims died in the summer of 1995. He had not been there during that time. 'But maybe the Muslims were fighting among themselves,' he eventually said. 'Maybe some Serbs wanted revenge. Anyway, what has happened, has happened.'

In 1974 Karadžić won a literary scholarship to Columbia University in the United States. He spent ten months in the country and tried to see as much of it as he could, improving his English along the way. He travelled to the West Coast, making detours to the southern and northern states. He returned to Sarajevo at the end of summer 1975.

While he was in the States, members of his family still in Sarajevo were regularly questioned by officials from the Communist Party and the secret police. They wanted to know why he was there, what he was doing, when he would be back. There was a great deal of suspicion. His wife and daughter were eventually allowed to go and stay with Radovan for the last six weeks of his trip, but their son, two-year-old Sasa, had to remain in Yugoslavia as 'insurance'. Ljiljana and Sonja stayed with Radovan in New York. They remember that time with great fondness.

When the family returned they were questioned again. They believed they were being treated as pro-Western, potential enemies of the state. 'When my father got some kind of award, as a doctor or as a poet,' recalls Sonja, 'there always was some kind of problem why they couldn't give that award. There were too many problems, small problems, but too many.'

The family also believes they were being spied upon by neighbours and friends. At dinner parties they would talk about their experiences in America. Their supposed friends would then go and report what was said. Sonja and Ljiljana say they only found out about this years later when the war began.

Meanwhile Radovan's career took something of a sporting turn. In 1978 he worked for three months as the team psychiatrist for the most prestigious football team in Yugoslavia, Red Star Belgrade. Later, he would continue the role with Sarajevo football club.

On 4 May 1980 Josip 'Broz' Tito died. He had held Yugoslavia together through a mixture of fear, political suppression and economic liberalism. He had managed to bury, to a certain extent, the raw emotions and ethnic hatreds that had characterised the conflict within the region during the Second World War and impose his own philosophy of 'brotherhood and unity'. It would not long survive his passing.

In 1982 Karadžić's aspiring literary career received a boost when he won the prestigious Branko Ćopić literary prize for a children's book.

In 1984 he tried to cash in on the biggest sporting event ever to have taken place in Yugoslavia: the Sarajevo Winter Olympics. With the benefit of hindsight, it was to be Bosnia's high watermark before the descent into chaos. To the joy and delight of all its citizens, Bosnia showed off its beautiful mountains and ski resorts for the whole world to see. Many will best remember the Sarajevo Olympics for the triumph of the British figure-skating partners, Torville and Dean, who danced to 'Bolero' to score maximum points.

Like many others, Karadžić sought to make the most of the imminent arrival of thousands of foreigners to the ski slopes of Jahorina, Igman and Bjelašnica. The Karadžić family had plans to build a motel, but various logistical problems prevented the scheme being achieved in time for the Games so alternative business proposals were considered. One of them was to begin producing mushrooms; another to farm chickens. These business initiatives came to nothing. The family claims the failure could be blamed on one of their workers who was a police agent. Karadžić felt increasingly that he was being treated as some kind of dissident and that the authorities were looking for any opportunity to persecute him.

He found himself in deeper trouble when he became embroiled in a scheme with his friend and future close political ally, Momčilo Krajišnik, who was employed in a state construction company. Krajišnik did some work for Karadžić; the family claim this was as a private individual and not on behalf of the construction company. The authorities decided to investigate the case and Karadžić was ultimately sentenced for his role. He spent eleven months in jail. The family maintains to this day that he did nothing wrong.

Meanwhile the Winter Olympics came and went. They were regarded as a huge success. But it was the last great show for Sarajevo, for Bosnia, and for Yugoslavia.

I talked to a man who was living on the outskirts of Sarajevo in a half-built house that leaked whenever it rained. He was 40 years old but looked much older. His health was bad. But worse than that were the nightmares. He often woke up in the middle of the night, screaming at the memory of dragging mutilated bodies from a river. Rotted limbs had come away in his hands. As he spoke, he rocked back on forth on the sofa. His wife and young son sat silently beside him.

After he was captured, he was taken to a camp where people

had to sleep on concrete floors. The camp commander would not let in the Red Cross. The guards beat them regularly. Suddenly he stood up in front of me and dragged a chair towards him, kneeling on it to expose the soles of his feet.

This is how they used to make me sit. They used police sticks and wooden poles to beat my feet. Afterwards, I could only walk on my knees. Sometimes, even today, the pain comes to my feet and I cannot walk. On another occasion, I was taken into the woods blindfolded, my hands tied behind my back. They loaded their guns as if they were going to shoot me. But nothing happened and we all went back to the camp.

He also remembered how, in the middle of winter, a prisoner was escorted naked into the cold and the guards poured freezing water over him: 'And there was sexual abuse as well. It happened many times.'

He was released four months after the war ended. Today he is unable to work because of his poor health. He has heart problems, experiences difficulty sleeping, and his short-term memory is bad. He sometimes forgets where he lives. He says he has no future.

In the hilltop cemetery of Topčider overlooking Belgrade it was time for the burial of another Serbian leader. Ivan Stambolić's remains had only recently been found on a hill outside the northern city of Novi Sad. He had been the Yugoslav political leader who had facilitated the rise of Slobodan Milošević during the 1980s before he himself was cast aside by his former protégé. Stambolić had been kidnapped while out jogging in August 2000. His remains were found in a pit of quicklime in March 2003. He had been shot. The chief suspects were once again members of the Red Berets.

Flurries of snow spun in the freezing air. I felt as if I was on some big Hollywood set, waiting for the key scene. Amidst the snow-covered trees family, friends and senior politicians had gathered to say farewell to the moderate politician who had tried his best to keep Yugoslavia together but had, unwittingly, been a conduit to its destruction. He had failed to stop Milošević leading the country down the path to war.

The State of Emergency was still in force following the murder of Zoran Djindjic. Police were present in large numbers at the approaches to the cemetery but we managed to persuade them to let us pass and join the other media already gathered near the outdoor chapel. I found myself next to the carriage that was being used to transport the coffin. A few paces away was a military guard of honour, perhaps 50 soldiers, young and fresh-faced, with their bayonets fixed.

The new Serbian Prime Minister, Zoran Živković, and the Prime Minister of Montenegro, Milo Djukanović, were among the mourners. They stood on the other side of the gun carriage, shaking hands with family members. It struck me again just how vulnerable they all were, even here, to the assassin's bullet. We had not been searched when we entered the graveyard. If anyone had wanted to carry out another killing, it would not have been difficult. The cold was bitter and, as soon as the formalities were over, I retreated quickly to the warmth of the car parked at the bottom of the hill. As I started the engine, I wondered if the forces responsible for the demise of Stambolić and Djindjic could be the same ones that were protecting Karadžić?

The two most respected institutions in Serbia were the Orthodox Church and the army. The latter had maintained very close links with its counterpart in Republika Srpska, the Bosnian Serb Army. It had been rumoured for some time that one of these armies – or both of them – had been protecting Ratko Mladić. In Bosnia, reform of the military had been hampered by the fact that there were two armies: the Muslim-Croat and the Bosnian Serb. But towards the end of 2003 there was a major breakthrough. Agreement in principle was made to merge them. A national Defence Ministry would be set up and there would be a central command. Soldiers would wear the same uniform, swear the same oath and serve under the same flag. For the first time ultimate control would rest with the state Presidency.

Although there was agreement on paper, I was curious to see whether this would actually work in practice, especially since the Bosnian Serb military was believed still to be protecting its former commander, General Mladić. I made a request to visit a Bosnian Serb Army base. To my surprise, the usually ultra suspicious authorities agreed.

The army base was just a few kilometres from Srebrenica, across a river, hidden among trees. As we entered the complex I was a little apprehensive. We were greeted by two stern looking soldiers. But I was given a tour of the facilities and invited to meet and interview whomever I wished. My guide was the regional commander – slightly overweight and wearing a perpetual smile. He showed me into the main administrative block, led me to a room and indicated that I should sit in one of the now familiar fake black leather armchairs. He introduced me to a couple of his lower-ranking officers and then proceeded to dispel virtually every prejudice I had relating to the RS military. Whether he had just been on a crash course with Saatchi & Saatchi, I never did discover. He admitted that 'there had been a crime at Srebrenica', and stated that he wanted his army to join NATO's Partnership for Peace Programme and, ultimately, even NATO itself.

This, surely, was heresy. After all, it was NATO who had bombed the Serbs into submission in 1995 and again, more recently, during the war in Kosovo. But that was what he said. It was a sign, perhaps, that the mood was changing in Bosnia. There was a growing sense of realism everywhere, but especially in the RS, an awareness that nationalism was one thing; putting bread and butter on the table was another. Years had passed since the end of the war but the economy was still not improving. There was little investment in either education or the military. The commander's men needed new uniforms, better equipment and training, and these would not be provided by clinging to the old tenets of nationalism and ethnic division.

The changing mood was also reflected in the Bosnian Serb police. About this time they carried out their own, independent mission to capture Karadžić. They had received a tip-off that the former President had been seen in the north-eastern town of Bijeljina. A raid was carried out on the local Serbian Orthodox Bishop's house but, if Karadžić had been there, he was long gone.

And then another funeral, this time of the wartime Muslim President of Bosnia, Alija Izetbegović. He had perhaps emerged with the cleanest hands of the three key leaders of the former Yugoslavia, who also included Franjo Tudjman in Croatia and Slobodan Milošević in Serbia, though the Serbs blamed Izetbegović as much as anyone for the war. As far as the Muslims were concerned, he had not perhaps been the ideal leader for wartime but was probably the best option they'd had.

For the first year since 1914, Sarajevo experienced snow in October. By the time the funeral took place it had turned to torrential rain. 'The heavens are crying,' some people claimed. But it did not stop more than 100,000 people turning out to pay their last respects. The procession wound around Sarajevo's city centre until the coffin was laid down outside the still bombed out Parliament building, opposite the Holiday Inn. Two huge flags hung from the windows of the government offices. I was totally caught up in the crush. We were all drenched. Speeches and prayers were read. And then, hesitantly at first but swelled by the thousands who joined in, a single chant rose from the masses.

'*Allāhu Akbar! Allāhu Akbar!*'

God is great, God is great!

6

Hunters

'I told you already that I don't know where he lives. I really don't know. And what the media writes, I can neither confirm nor deny. I simply don't know' – Ljiljana Karadžić speaking to the author, 9 March 2004

My plane bumped down on the icy runway at Sarajevo airport. Marko was waiting for me, the car engine running. He stubbed out his cigarette and off we went as fast as was reasonably possible on the treacherous road to Pale. On the descent towards the town, after the final tunnel, I could see German armoured vehicles blocking the road ahead. Razor wire was stretched across the road and German soldiers were standing about in their winter camouflage, rifles at the ready.

I had cut short my vacation in the UK after receiving urgent news from Bosnia. 'If you don't come now,' I was told, 'you will regret it for the rest of your career.' My source was linked to the foreign military presence in Bosnia. He was high-level and had access to restricted information. I had to take his advice seriously.

It was well known that domestic and foreign intelligence services were monitoring calls through increasingly advanced interception systems. The CIA, in particular, had a vast operation in Bosnia, and other interested parties had their own quota of agents and electronic listening capacity in the country. If they were not spying on local criminals or politicians, they were spying on each other. Journalists' contacts were an obvious group to monitor. It was always risky to be too precise on the phone, so I used a simple code that meant basic information could be exchanged without compromising my sources. They would ring me and say something like: 'How's it going? What's happening? You know, we should really go to that bar sometime. I think it's an absolute must. Yes, the one in . . .' That would be code for the fact that some information related to Karadžić that had recently come out or, was about to come out, was good and would be worth my while pursuing. The location of the bar would be where the raid would take place. Or, alternatively, the source might say something like, 'I really wouldn't be seen dead in that place. No way.' Which would mean, do not bother with that information, it is totally inaccurate. It was hardly sophisticated, but it worked on a number of occasions. My source's identity was protected and I had a crucial tip-off.

The problem I had with this particular call was that I did not really know the individual in question and had set up no such code. But instinct told me I should return to Bosnia as soon as possible. I could not afford to miss out if the information was accurate. Begging a lift from a friend, I headed straight to Heathrow airport, booking a plane ticket on the way. I telephoned Marko, my 'fixer', to make arrangements for my arrival.

As I rushed to the airport, I made a number of calls to try to establish what had led to all the recent speculation that the former Bosnian Serb President had been arrested. Apparently, on the Friday night, NATO in Bosnia had received information that Karadžić was seeking medical attention in Pale. It was thought he had a knee problem. In driving snow and a bitter wind, Italian Carabinieri units had been despatched immediately from Sarajevo. They were now in the process of raiding a number of premises in the town, including the hospital, a Red Cross facility and some private houses.

As we descended the hill with the German roadblock in front of us, I noticed that a group of journalists was gathered at a nearby petrol station, so we pulled up next to them. A NATO spokesman informed us that the German armoured personnel carriers were sealing off the town, blocking all approach roads, setting up checkpoints and searching all vehicles coming in and out. I waited until he had finished then grabbed his elbow and eased him away from the media pack.

'Have you got him?'

'Well . . . it's an ongoing operation and . . .'

'Have you got him?'

'Er . . . no. At least, not yet.'

Getting back into the car, we travelled down to the famous 'Pink House' where Karadžić's wife and daughter and sister-in-law were living. Along the way we saw NATO troops and more armoured vehicles positioned at various strategic locations in the town. The search of the Pink House had already taken place. As we approached it, I could see three Italian Carabinieri officers, in their dark blue uniforms and black balaclavas, standing menacingly in front of the gate which was the only entry point. A two-metre-high wall surrounded the house and garden.

Although feeling bitterly disappointed that my speedy return had been rewarded with a false alarm, I dutifully asked the Carabinieri officers if I could take a picture of them for the news website I was working for. They talked amongst themselves for a minute, then one of them told me in broken English that it would be OK. I walked back a few paces, went down on one knee and began to focus my lens. As I did so, I noticed the three of them moving closer together and then, in a flurry of movement, they whipped off their balaclavas, linked arms and beamed for the camera. Not quite the dramatic news shot I was looking for. Nevertheless I took a couple of shots before suggesting that it would be nice to have a few more with them in their original position and balaclavas on.

Afterwards I went in search of a senior commander. He told me that they had had a '100 per cent certain sighting of Karadžić' in the last few days, but could not supply any further details. He compared the hunt for Karadžić with that for Saddam Hussein (who had finally been captured the previous month in a hole in the ground, somewhere in Iraq).

'We got Saddam through his support network. We're doing the same here,' the commander told me. 'We have clear evidence that he contacted his family and his inner support network.' I was still not convinced. But I duly waited around in the snow with other journalists for a while longer and eventually a statement was brought out from Ljiljana Karadžić: 'They [referring to SFOR] have been looking for my husband in the walls, in every inch of the house, and even in the septic tank. They seem to believe Radovan would hide like Saddam Hussein.' But they had not found him. I asked my fixer to drive me back to Sarajevo; there was no point in staying here any longer.

A long traffic jam led back towards the garage and the German checkpoint. Every single vehicle was being method-ically searched. My driver asked me if I would prefer to get back to Sarajevo more quickly. I looked at him, surprised, and said, 'Of course!' He reversed the car a few metres, made a U-turn, drove along the main highway for a short time then suddenly turned off on to a smaller road. Five minutes later, we rejoined the main highway – beyond the German check-point. Our short detour had taken us through a few back streets on the edge of Pale. I was astounded. SFOR had said they had totally sealed off the town, that all approach roads were covered and no one could get in or out without passing SFOR troops. Yet we had just circumnavigated all the roadblocks and checkpoints in Pale in a matter of minutes. It made the much-vaunted security look like a complete shambles.

The next day I rang the spokesperson for NATO and told him what we had done. There was a long pause, then he asked how we had managed it. After I gave him the details, he said he would get back to me. A few minutes later he rang back and claimed that the particular road I had taken was being 'observed' at the time. It was all part of the operation. I pointed out that simply 'observing' the road would hardly have prevented Karadžić, or anyone else for that matter, from hiding in the boot of a car and being driven out. There was another pause. Then slowly, and most unconvincingly, he assured me

Radovan Karadžić explains an ethnic map of Bosnia-Herzegovina to journalists at his headquarters in Pale, January 1993. (Getty Images)

Ratko Mladić, the commander of Bosnian Serb forces, arriving at Sarajevo airport to negotiate the withdrawal of his troops from Mount Igman, August 1993. After the war, he is believed to have spent much of his time on the run in Serbia. (AFP/Getty Images)

Victims of the Srebrenica massacre are buried in the memorial cemetery at Potočari.

Petnica, the village in Montenegro where Radovan Karadžić was born.

Muslim prisoners at the Omarska camp in northern Bosnia-Herzegovina, August 1992.
This was one of a number of detention centres run by the Bosnian Serbs during the war.
(AP Photo/ITN)

(*Facing page*) The funeral of Serbian Prime Minister Zoran Djindjić, assassinated in the centre of Belgrade on 12 March 2003. 500,000 people attended his funeral. (Reuters/CORBIS)

(*Above*) Carabinieri outside the Karadžić Pink House in Pale.

(*Below*) Ljiljana Karadžić. Picture taken by the author at the Pink House in Pale.

A shelled-out building in the centre of Sarajevo, May 1992. (AP Photo/ David Brauchli)

The author interviewing Carla Del Ponte in Belgrade, June 2007.

Paddy Ashdown, the High Representative to Bosnia 2002–2006. He believed a more co-ordinated approach was needed to track down Karadžić.

Metropolitan Amfilohije Radovic from the Serbian Orthodox Church. A strong supporter of the Karadžić family.

The burial of Jovanka Karadžić, Nikšić, Montenegro, 7 May 2005. Spies looking for Karadžić were among the mourners.

that the road was definitely known to NATO forces who were closely monitoring it. I put the phone down on him.

Over the next few hours the operation was downsized and SFOR troops began returning to barracks. Everyone, including the media, thought it was all over. But that night a second raid was launched on another building in Pale – this time the official former residence of the Karadžić family.

The Pink House was not the official family home. That was a big white house at a place called Krivaca on the outskirts of the town, set back from the main street behind a screen of trees. Karadžić and members of his family were believed to have lived here in the years immediately after the Bosnian War, in 1996–7. A number of his bodyguards used to patrol at the entrance. These days the house was believed to be empty and only a single security guard remained to keep an eye on the premises. During the initial SFOR raids on the town, a number of documents had been seized and one man had been detained, accused of helping war crimes fugitives. SFOR claimed the raid on the house in Krivaca was a direct result of information obtained during the preceding days.

In the early hours of the morning, SFOR troops went to Pale police station and took a couple of Bosnian Serb policemen to Krivaca. What happened next is the subject of a dispute between the security guard at the house, the Karadžić family and SFOR. According to the former, the two Bosnian Serb policemen were used as human shields and pushed in front of the SFOR troops as they approached the house, fearing that anyone inside could open fire. The SFOR troops then kicked in the front door. (This story was subsequently denied by SFOR.)

Once inside, the SFOR troops appear to have carried out an 'over-enthusiastic' search. According to the Karadžić family, the soldiers deliberately wrecked the interior: ripping a treasured family icon with a knife, destroying a corner sofa and damaging windows and doors. They also assembled a bizarre exhibition of various items that they found. According to the family these included an old, traditional Montenegrin cap, paintings from the basement and some maps – all carefully laid out as if they were to be photographed. The family estimated that the damage caused amounted to about 10,000 Bosnian Marks (€5,000), about the same amount of damage as was inflicted on the Pink House. In the days that followed the Karadžićs began proceedings to sue NATO over the raids. I interviewed the spokesperson for the local Bosnian Serb police and he confirmed that the the family had formally filed charges, and said that, yes, two of their policemen had, in effect, been used as human shields during the raid.

Carla Del Ponte, Chief Prosecutor at The Hague Tribunal, claimed that Karadžić had been in Pale at the time of the first raid but SFOR troops had arrived 'two hours too late'. But she provided no hard evidence to back up these claims. The failure of the operation, and the subsequent embarrassment for NATO, could not be denied, while the mystique of the former Bosnian Serb leader was only enhanced. He appeared to be untouchable.

After the botch-up in Pale I spoke to Western security sources, people linked to The Hague Tribunal, and to other journalists who were following the story. One person told me that the raid had all been a public relations stunt for the new US General in charge of SFOR and that they had known all along that Karadžić was not there. Another suggested the operation was carried out as a result of deliberate disinformation on the part of Karadžić's support network, the idea being that while SFOR troops were focussing their attention on Pale, Karadžić used the opportunity to slip across the border into Serbia, hundreds of kilometres away. Someone else told me it was more complicated than I realised; that it was very difficult to understand what motivated SFOR because SFOR itself should not be seen as a single, cohesive peacekeeping force. That might be how it appeared on the surface and in the public eye but the truth was that individual nations kept important information to themselves and reported to their own national military structures before dealing with SFOR. He said there were petty jealousies and rivalries between the different countries, and private alliances within the umbrella organisation. The Americans and British had close links, although the former by no means shared all the information they had with the latter.

Confused by all the conflicting information, I had lunch with one of Lord Ashdown's advisers. He admitted that there was a lack of hard intelligence on Karadžić's whereabouts. As for the Americans, he believed they wanted to wrap up the Karadžić issue once and for all so that they could 'pack their bags, declare victory and leave Bosnia'.

According to my lunch companion, the one thing that Karadžić really feared was being betrayed by his own people. Somehow, the hunters had to persuade the hard-line Serbs that it was in their interests to give up their former leader. The big question was: carrot or stick? Perhaps the stick would be more effective: issuing political ultimatums and carrying out the threats if necessary. He told me how they had tried to persuade Western governments to supply resources to help capture Karadžić while the conflict with Iraq was in full swing. They argued that, as the West was being accused of being 'anti-Muslim' in Iraq, they could balance this by showing that they were genuinely trying to find, and bring to justice to Karadžić – a man accused of genocide against Muslims.

As to Karadžić's current whereabouts, he repeated the familiar theory that he was probably somewhere in the remote mountains of South Bosnia, frequently crossing the nearby border into Montenegro.

A week later I went to one of the buildings owned by the United States Embassy. It was widely believed, with some justification, that little of any significance happened in Bosnia without the say-so of Uncle Sam. I was to meet two senior embassy officials for an 'off the record' interview. After a frustrating half-hour of semantic argument which, at one point, focussed on what was meant by the word 'is', I established absolutely nothing beyond the earth-shattering insight that Karadžić had probably remained free for so long because he had a very good support network. But I did receive confirmation that not all the organisations involved in the hunt were working together and sharing information.

I had already decided that it was time for me to try and interview members of the Karadžić family. I had been circling the issue for some time, knowing they were reluctant to speak to the media, especially the Western media which was generally regarded with deep suspicion. I had no telephone numbers for the family and the danger of going direct to the Pink House was that I might simply be ignored. And then I had a piece of luck. On a second trip to Pale in the days immediately following the abortive raids, I decided to get my car washed.

As I sat chatting with my fixer in the small coffee shop attached to the garage, I noticed a leaflet lying on the table. Out of simple curiosity, I asked Marko what it said. 'It's advertising a business,' he said. 'And guess what? It's run by Sonja Karadžić, Radovan's daughter.' The company was called Komplemedik Centar and it specialised in alternative therapies. I asked my fixer to translate the leaflet. It transpired that a series of alternative medical treatments were being offered, including acupuncture, psychotherapy, 'bioptron zepter therapy' and a 'fotomedical anti-cellulite programme', whatever the last two were. A very generous discount of 20 per cent was being offered as a promotion. At the bottom of the leaflet was a mobile telephone number. People interested in learning more about the Komplemedik Centar or wishing to make an appointment were invited to call.

I took a deep breath and dialled. After a few rings the phone was answered. It was Sonja, but when she learned that I was a journalist she said she would only talk to my interpreter. I passed the phone to Marko and, through him, asked a few questions. I first wanted to know if she would do an interview. She said she did not have time because she was making cookies for her children. I then asked her what she thought about the NATO raids. She said she was furious. 'We are the only family in the world where these raids can take place without there being any consequences for those who carried them out,' she told me. She also confirmed that the family would sue NATO. Just as I thought I was getting somewhere, Marko shook his head silently in my direction and then pulled the phone away from his ear. Apparently, the cookies were threatening to burn and she had gone to deal with them.

At 10.30 a.m. on Saturday 6 March I had my first proper conversation with a member of the Karadžić family. I used the telephone number from the alternative medical centre leaflet again. Sonja picked up the phone. I asked whether she and her mother would allow me to interview them. In good English, she told me firmly that she would discuss it with her mother and they would get back to me.

Radovan Karadžić emerged from prison in autumn 1985. He returned to the flat on Sutjeska Street in Sarajevo, opposite the school his daughter Sonja was attending. The afterglow of the Olympics was fading and Yugoslavia was already beginning to unravel. People once more began to talk with pride about being Serb or Croat or Muslim. In 1983, the Muslim leader Alija Izetbegović and a dozen associates had been sent to jail, accused of plotting to create 'an ethnically pure Muslim Bosnia-Herzegovina'. Despite serious doubts about the veracity of the charges, Izetbegović was sentenced to 14 years in prison but served less than five. During the Bosnian War, his opponents claimed that he was trying to impose a strict form of Islam on the country.

In September 1986 extracts from a document written by the Serbian Academy of Sciences and Arts were published in a Serbian newspaper. The so-called Memorandum *was a political bombshell, warning that the Serb nation was under threat, that Yugoslavia was disintegrating and Serbs in Croatia were in danger again, all of which reignited memories of World War II when the Nazi-backed fascists in Croatia had system-atically massacred thousands and thousands of Serbs. Dobrica Ćosić, the Serbian writer and thinker whom Karadžić had first met in the 1960s, defended the* Memorandum *and enhanced his position as a leading light of the Serbian nationalist intelligentsia.*

After his jail term, Karadžić decided to go to Belgrade, believing it would be a better place to pursue a career as a psychiatrist and writer. Ljiljana said he chose Belgrade not because it was a Serbian city but simply because it was the largest in Yugoslavia and offered the most opportunities. 'The population was changing,' she said. 'The older people who were originally from Sarajevo were gradually dying out and they were increasingly being replaced by people from Kosovo or the Sandžak (a mainly Muslim region of Serbia). Croats moved to Croatia, Serbs to Serbia, and people were concerned about these developments. In the cafes and hotels it was not the same atmosphere.' But whatever the demographic changes in Sarajevo, they were hardly cause for war.

Returning to Sarajevo after his period away, Karadžić began to dabble in politics. He flirted first with the Green Party. His wife describes this as a 'little episode' in his life. But politics was beginning to take a front seat in many people's lives by then. Slobodan Milošević came to power in Serbia as nationalism began to take hold in Croatia, exemplified by the founding of the Croatian Democratic Union (HDZ) by Franjo Tudjman in June 1989. The old Yugoslav Socialism was becoming less attractive. People were seeking both a sense of identity and protection by supporting the parties that represented their own nationality. Memories of World War II also helped fuel a new cycle of fear and paranoia. The politics of ethnic division flourished. In Bosnia, the mainly Muslim Party of Democratic Action (SDA) was founded on 26 May 1990 by, among others, Alija Izetbegović.

The Karadžićs hosted regular gatherings at their home in Sarajevo, inviting other prominent Serbs to discuss how to respond to this changing political environment. They discussed the creation of a new party and considered who would lead it in the light of Bosnia's first free elections, scheduled to take place in November 1990.

Ljiljana Karadžić claimed her husband was not a nationalist but that he was becoming increasingly worried about the situation of the Serbs in Bosnia. She said her husband did not initially want to be the leader of the new Serbian Democratic Party (SDS), but was happy simply to be a member of its ruling board. Others were approached only to turn the big job down. Finally Radovan Karadžić was elected.

While many still believed that multi-ethnic, multi-cultural Sarajevo would hold firm, the war in Croatia was already radicalising people. Sarajevo was not yet affected but it could only be a matter of time before Radovan Karadžić would find himself at the head of a Serbian war machine, determined to oppose the creation of the independent state of Bosnia Herzegovina – at any cost.

The first few weeks of 2004 saw a flurry of activity by SFOR and other international bodies in Bosnia. There were the raids in Pale, more raids on the Karadžić-owned Sveti Jovan (St John) radio station, also in Pale, and on a telecommunications centre. More people were detained by SFOR, including a former Republika Srpska Defence Minister, and alleged helpers of Karadžić had their assets frozen. On 11 February Carla Del Ponte stated categorically that Karadžić was living in Belgrade and could be arrested and transferred to The Hague 'tomorrow' if there was the political will. But, she said, there was not. Again she produced no hard evidence, no address, no photograph to prove her allegations. It was a simple matter for the authorities in Belgrade once again to deny the charges.

A senior Western diplomat in Sarajevo told me that he felt Del Ponte's statement was 'not helpful'. He described her as acting 'like a bull in a china shop'. Del Ponte was not the most popular of individuals within diplomatic circles. But, significantly, he did not deny the substance of what she had said. I suspected that he believed she might well be right. The diplomat told me that those hunting Karadžić believed he had several layers of protection – he likened these to concentric circles. The innermost circle contained only a very few people, his absolutely loyal lieutenants. The outer circles provided logistical support. People from different circles barely had any contact with each other, in order to maintain security. But, again, there was no hard evidence of any of this.

Meanwhile, my request for an interview with the Karadžić family had finally been granted. I headed back to the famous Pink House. It was one of those dirty days you sometimes get in Bosnia as winter melts into spring and the once-pristine snow dissolves into a brown mush, polluted by car exhaust fumes. Potholed roads, poor drainage and appalling conditions combined to produce that uniquely Bosnian driving experience. Low grey cloud and intermittent drizzle only enhanced the depressing atmosphere. I met the intermediary who would introduce me to the family in one of the shiny bars on the outskirts of the town. At a pre-arranged time Sonja rang and asked if we could pick her up outside the local school.

We drove to the rendezvous and Sonja got in the front passenger seat next to me. I followed her directions. As we approached the Pink House, the road deteriorated into a dirt track. I parked outside the gate where, two months earlier, the Carabinieri had posed for photographs, in and out of their balaclavas. Entering the house through the garden ahead of Sonja, I was immediately confronted by a wheaten-coloured dog which came bounding up, wagging its tail.

'This is my dog,' Sonja told me, with a big smile.

In a sitting room on the first floor, I was introduced to Ljiljana and, briefly, to her sister whose arm appeared to be broken and was in a sling.

I took a seat on the sofa while mother and daughter prepared a drink in the kitchen, which was an extension of the living room. The walls were painted yellow and the soft furnishings had a floral design. I noticed a picture of Saint Nicholas and on top of the TV set stood a clock with the emblem of the Red Cross. Ljiljana used to work for them. A stack of news-papers and magazines covered a coffee table in the centre of the room.

Sonja was wearing a voluminous purple blouse with, dis-concertingly, lipstick to match. She talked fast and cheerfully. Ljiljana seemed more reserved at first. She wore her dark hair pulled back from her face. She was wearing a long black dress and a red jacket, nails neatly painted red also. There was a long gold chain around her neck that reached halfway down her front. Half a dozen large imitation pearls were attached to it.

We chatted for around three-quarters of an hour before starting the official interview. Sonja spoke English much better than her mother, who made the excuse that too many bad articles had been written in that language about her family. As time passed the atmosphere between us relaxed, with Sonja always deferring to her mother. Talk ranged from the causes of the war, to Radovan's time in the United States during the 1970s, to family birthdays.

'Where is your husband?' I asked suddenly, looking Ljiljana straight in the eye.

'I would love to know where he is,' she replied. 'I really don't know because that way, he, his guards and we, his family, are protected – especially when we are being followed and when we're put in these unpleasant situations. It is better that we do not know.'

'When was the last time you had contact with him?'

'A long time ago – almost four years. It shouldn't mean anything to you because it was quick and it was a personal thing. Even my children did not know. And since then we haven't seen each other at all.'

'What impression did you have of him?'

'Well, he's always been an optimist, a cheerful person. He's a psychiatrist by profession, and that means when he is in a crisis he knows how to help himself.'

'Some in the international community accuse you of protecting him. Are you?'

'First, we are Radovan's family and, clearly, as members of the family, we would do everything to protect him. But we are not in a position to give him any protection.'

Ljiljana then claimed her husband had said he had reached a deal with the leading American negotiator, Richard Holbrooke, who had helped broker the end of the Bosnian War in 1995.

'In fact, Radovan told me that Mr Holbrooke was pressing him to withdraw from the Presidency of Republika Srpska and his party, and to withdraw from public life. He said that Holbrooke had also said that the charges against him would be withdrawn, he wouldn't be pursued and that he could forget about The Hague.'

It was an allegation I had heard before, the same one I had put to ex-President Clinton myself in the cemetery in Srebrenica, but now I was hearing the claims first-hand from somebody at the centre of events at the time.

'When was the deal done?'

'I think it was in the spring of 1996. I cannot remember the exact date because there was a series of meetings and agreements, but Radovan stepped down on the thirtieth of June 1996.'

'These allegations have been denied. What evidence do you have that a deal was done?'

'I don't have the document and I've not seen it. But I know there was no reason for him to step down otherwise.'

The same old problem: hearsay, rumour, no hard evidence.

'Can you contact your husband if you want to?'

'No. Imagine how many times I wanted to contact him in the last four years.'

'Do you know where he is?'

'I don't know. I really don't know.'

I had outstayed my welcome. As we left the living room, Sonja said that during the last SFOR raid on the house a soldier had measured the wall, in front and behind, to calculate whether there were any hidden rooms between the kitchen and the bathroom. Apparently, they did not find any.

Three days later, a new front was opened in the campaign to arrest the war crimes fugitives. It was 12 March and the birthday of Karadžić's former army chief, Ratko Mladić. A full page advertisement had been taken out in the main Bosnian newspaper. There was a picture of a set of handcuffs. Around it was written: '*Ratko nismo zaboravili. Jedini poklon.*' (Ratko, we haven't forgotten. The only present.) And then, at the bottom of the page, one word: 'Uskoro' (Almost).

This marked a stepping up of the war criminals pursuit. With no apparent success in their ground campaign, SFOR and other agencies were adopting a new tactic: psychological pressure.

7

Explosions and Failure

'The operation was conducted based on information indicating that Radovan Karadžić was going to be present in a specific location . . . factors beyond our control resulted in the tragic injury of two civilians' – NATO (SFOR) statement on the failed arrest operation, 2 April 2004

It was around one o'clock in the morning. I was lying in bed in the Hotel Moscow in central Belgrade when my mobile phone suddenly burst into life. I fumbled for the answer button. A worried voice came on the line.

'Listen, it's me. I know it's late but I have a bit of a problem. I have a British soldier standing in front of me and he's pointing a rifle at my stomach. He's not very happy . . . looks a bit twitchy. I was hoping you might be able to have a word with him, explain who I am and what I'm doing. It's a bit tense.'

It was my contact in Pale.

'What's happened? Where are you?'

'There's been another raid . . . explosions, gunfire . . . it's a hell of a mess. I'm standing outside the priest's house in Pale.'

Another voice came on the line then. The man had a broad Yorkshire accent.

'All right, mate, who's that?'

I gave him my details.

'Yeah, well, who's this bloke? He's not allowed round 'ere. Is he one of yours?'

'Yes, he's working for me. He's OK, don't worry. Sorry for any inconvenience.'

'Yeah . . . well, that's all right then. As long as he stays clear of the 'ouse.'

The line went dead. Two minutes later, the phone rang again and my contact was back on the phone, explaining what had happened. He had been having a drink in a bar in Pale, about a kilometre away from the town centre, when he heard an almighty explosion. Seconds later he had received a phone call from a friend who had been close to the blast. There appeared to be some sort of military operation underway near the priest's house. My contact had jumped in his car and driven there imme-diately to see what was happening. In the centre of town there was a Serbian Orthodox church and priest's house, a small park surrounding both. The whole area had been cordoned off by SFOR soldiers.

According to eyewitnesses, just after midnight a vehicle resembling an ice cream van had passed through the centre of Pale. People noticed it because ice cream vans were not a common sight there (or in Bosnia, for that matter), and they were definitely not a common sight around midnight. A short time later there had been a number of explosions and, some claimed, gunfire, in the vicinity of the house. There was a lot of shouting and a few minutes later dark figures were seen leaving the priest's house. Almost at the same time, British troops arrived and formed a cordon around the area. Witnesses said they had also seen Slovenian and American troops. Already rumours were circulating that it was Karadžić they were looking for. Nobody knew if they had been successful or not.

Pacing my hotel room, 300 kilometres away, there was not a lot I could do. It was now 2.30 a.m. I decided to get dressed, go to the office and file the story, hedging my bets as to what the aim of the raid had been and whether it had been successful or not. As I walked the short distance I made calls to various contacts in Sarajevo, to try to get a fuller picture of the night's events.

The next day it emerged there had indeed been an attempt

to capture Karadžić but it had gone disastrously wrong. The explosion had been caused by plastic explosive placed on various doors and walls of the priest's house. The idea was to disable temporarily any of the fugitive's bodyguards who might be inside. Neither Karadžić nor his bodyguards had in fact been there, but the blast had been so severe that the local priest had been taken to hospital and was now in a coma. His son had also been admitted with severe injuries.

SFOR released a statement:

The operation was conducted based on information indicating that Radovan Karadžić was going to be present in a specific location in Pale on 1 April. Neither the church nor the clergy were the focus of this operation and the church itself was not entered by SFOR personnel. Our initial review of the operation has indicated that the design of the ground floor channelled and thus magnified the overpressure [of the blast]. It appears that their injuries were solely the result of the blast. This was a completely unintended and deeply unfortunate consequence of the device that could not have been anticipated.

But the damage had been done. All the familiar criticisms about the West being anti-Serb, insensitive towards the Serbian Church, and recklessly heavy-handed, now resurfaced in the Serbian media. Within hours demonstrations were organised to protest against the raid. For foreigners, Pale once again became a risky place to be and international organisations based in Sarajevo warned their employees not to travel to the town.

During the next few days I rang round my contacts to find out what had really happened. I was told by two separate sources that the operation had been carried out by special forces from a European country. The British troops present on the evening were part of SFOR and had been sent there to provide a cordon around the area. A Special Forces unit from a European country had then been sent in.

By 2004 there were no special forces from any Western nation routinely stationed in Bosnia. They had been dispatched to other conflict zones, such as Afghanistan and Iraq. When these special forces had arrived in Bosnia, members of the Bosnian Serb security structures became aware of them very rapidly. It was possible, my source said, that Karadžić had been forewarned of unusual activity at the airport and had simply changed his plans. Yet again, an operation had been launched to find him and its results illustrated either the incompetence and inability of the West to catch him or else the superior intelligence or counter-intelligence of those who were protecting him.

Still smarting from the embarrassment of the failed raid, SFOR decided to go on the offensive. Another statement was issued explaining why, sometimes, 'force regrettably has to be used'. The statement continued:

There is a choice facing this country and time is running out. It is a simple choice: Karadžić or Europe. Karadžić means staying with the past: a web of crime, corruption and deceit that stifles any economic progress. Europe means the chance for jobs, to improve the standard of living for every citizen, the chance for Bosnia-Herzegovina to grow as a new European state. Radovan Karadžić is holding every citizen of this country hostage.

I had already been with Lord Ashdown to the region of Trebinje and seen for myself how difficult it was to monitor all the paths and other routes into Montenegro. Now I determined to see things from the perspective of the peacekeepers themselves with a trip to the region of Foča, regarded as one of the most hard-line Serb areas in Bosnia. It was the region to which many alleged war criminals were believed to have fled. Just after the war it was under French control. Relations between the French and the Serbs had always been better than between other nationalities. One French Ambassador to Bosnia had told me that there was an unspoken agreement among countries that when tough negotiations had to take place with the Serbs, the French would always be sent in because it was believed they would have more influence. But they were quick to deny any allegations of even tolerance of fugitives in their zone.

The SFOR peacekeepers were divided between different regions around Bosnia. In the countryside and mountains behind Foča there was a contingent of 200 German troops. Their stated aim was to maintain a 'safe and secure environment'. Even though there was no real major threat of renewed conflict between the ethnic groups, tensions remained simmering under the surface and it made sense to maintain a visible, if gradually decreasing, foreign military presence. But in this area German troops were warned to stay away from certain bars in the town, for fear of a hostile reaction from the locals, and their vehicles were occasionally stoned by local youths.

The German base was situated on an elevated piece of land just off the main road. The local commander gave me a tour of the camp and explained that of the 200 personnel under his command, only around half were combat troops. The rest were support staff, cooks, administrators. Their key role was to provide the 'blue box' in an arrest operation. This meant that his soldiers would cordon off large areas, to prevent the public from entering or leaving and also to provide support, if needed. Apparently there had been no German special forces in Bosnia for the past four years because they had been deployed on more urgent operations in Afghanistan.

Furthermore, under their own national legal code, German soldiers did not have the power actually to arrest anyone. So if Radovan Karadžić happened to be going for a stroll outside the base, they were powerless. Only 100 fighting men and an area of responsibility which covered some 1,700 square kilometres, including nine international border crossings of which just one was officially open during the winter because of the deep snow which blocked the roads. 'Actually, anyone can come and go,' I was told. 'There is nothing we can do to stop it. At one of the border crossings, the only thing marking the fact that you are at an international border is a sign nailed to a tree.' To make matters worse, the roads were in bad repair and often did not even appear on maps. The local population, of course, was distinctly hostile to NATO troops and, given the lie of the land, were in the perfect position to sound an early warning of any imminent NATO raid.

Senior Western officials, including those from NATO, had a habit of issuing upbeat statements implying the imminent arrest of Karadžić and other fugitives. In the first months of 2004, the Secretary-General of NATO Jaap de Hoop Scheffer, was quoted as saying: 'It is unacceptable that Karadžić is still at large. He may hide for a certain period but he cannot hide for ever.' Later he said, 'He can keep hiding but he cannot run forever. Everybody's doing everything they can to get him.' Other people talked about the 'Karadžić network being squeezed' and the 'noose around Karadžić's neck tightening'. But the truth of the matter was very different – as I witnessed with my visit to the German troops. There were simply not enough resources on the ground, and the resources that did exist were slowly being reduced as SFOR continued to down-size.

During the spring and summer of 2004 the United States suspended aid worth $25 million to Serbia because of the latter's failure to co-operate with The Hague; the assets of ten more individuals were frozen, including those of a former President of Bosnia, and more travel bans were introduced. Defending these strategies, Lord Ashdown said, 'Mr Karadžić heads a crime gang and we are responding accordingly.'

The Bosnian Serb police again carried out an operation to arrest Karadžić near the eastern Bosnian town of Bratunac, very close to Srebrenica. Special units using tracker dogs combed the area close to the border, following a tip-off that Karadžić was attempting to cross into Serbia. For 50 kilometres along the banks of the River Drina, separating Bosnian and Serbia, police checkpoints were established. The only criminals found were a few cattle rustlers and petty thieves. It was not clear whether the involvement of the RS police was simply an attempt to give the impression that they were co-operating with The Hague or whether it really was a genuine attempt to arrest their former

President. Either way, it was a sign that things were changing. The symbolism was extremely important.

While relations deteriorated between the international community and the Karadžić family and their supporters, my own personal contact with the family began to bear fruit. I found myself in the living room of the Pink House again. Business at Sonja's alternative medicine clinic seemed to be going well. Our conversation kept being interrupted by phone calls and, sitting on the other side of the room, was one of Sonja's actual patients, a young girl apparently suffering from a pollen allergy. Every few minutes Sonja would go over to her and insert or withdraw an acupuncture needle from her arm or ankle. It was not easy to conduct a conversation in these circumstances but I was determined to return to the subject of a possible deal between her father and the Americans.

In response, Ljiljana produced a letter which she claimed had been sent from Chicago, a city with a large number of Serb immigrants, many of whom retained strong nationalist feelings. The letter was anonymous, its only signature the word 'Friends'. Ljiljana drew my attention to a reference to the alleged Holbrooke-Karadžić deal and I noted the final message was 'don't trust the Americans'.

There was no way of knowing if the letter was real or a fabrication. The family had no other documents that confirmed any kind of deal. They had seen nothing themselves. But Ljiljana did suggest there were a few people who might be able to help me, former members of Karadžić's wartime inner cabinet, and one former senior official within the Milošević government. At least now I had something to work on.

After the interview they invited me to visit their Sveti Jovan radio station. In the main studio, opposite the control desk, hung a curtain. Sonja called me over and pulled this back to reveal a hospital bed behind which hung a chart of the human body, showing where acupuncture needles should be placed. With a big smile, she asked me if I would like to receive some treatment. I declined politely.

* * *

Two weeks later the Republika Srpska Government took another step in its efforts to resolve the war crimes issue. They announced that they would now be prepared to offer a financial package to those who gave themselves up and were prepared to go to The Hague. The package included cash payments, lawyer's fees, education scholarships for fugitive's children and free trips to The Hague for family members. Public opinion in Sarajevo was outraged by the move, but hardheaded Western diplomats were aware of the power of ready cash over the minds of many people and there was a general belief that this could be a very practical way of persuading fugitives to hand themselves in.

The psychological pressure was also stepped up. Following the full-page 'birthday advert' for Mladić in March, the same manoeuvre was repeated on 19 June to mark Karadžić's birthday, in Bosnia's biggest-selling daily newspaper. Above the picture of one silver candle was written 'Radovan, we have not forgotten'. Next to the candle was written 'The only [birthday] present'. And at the bottom of the page the word 'Almost'.

In the same month, the spokesperson for Carla Del Ponte, Florence Hartmann, appeared at a conference in Sarajevo. Afterwards I spoke to her about the current situation. I was aware that Del Ponte had something called a 'tracking team', but was not clear exactly what that was.

'We have had this team for two or three years,' Hartmann told me. 'Del Ponte insisted on having a tracking team almost from the first day she was in office in September 1999 because intelligence or information about the location of fugitives is the first step before an arrest . . . There are people coming to us with information, as surely as they are coming to other structures who are interested in locating fugitives.'

But The Hague did not have the power to arrest people themselves. They could only pass on this information to the relevant authorities – whether the security structures of a country or the international peacekeepers. Hartmann expressed a growing sense of frustration. 'For two and a half years, we were passing information to the authorities in Serbia regarding the location of Mladić. Nothing happened.' There was evident concern that SFOR itself might not be chasing up all the information. 'We pass information to SFOR and then it's up to them to check it, to assess the modality of further steps and even arrest. And it's not a problem if they miss a target in an operation. The important thing is to use the information as soon as possible because it might not be useful after a few hours, if it relates to the location of fugitives.'

'Has SFOR always checked what you passed on to them?'

'We do not have full feedback so I cannot assess if they are checking everything. It happened once that we believed we had some really good information [and passed it on] but we didn't see any further steps. Were there any further steps? I don't know, you should ask SFOR.'

In the summer of 1990 Karadžić and the Muslim leader Izetbegović went to a memorial ceremony for Serb and Muslim victims of World War II. The venue was the town of Foča where countless atrocities had been committed by the various warring factions during the 1940s. Both leaders said that 'blood must never flow down the Drina River ever again'. And Karadžić was reported as saying, 'Our Muslims are much closer to us [Bosnian Serbs] than many Christian peoples in Europe.'

But already a Serb rebellion had taken place in Croatia, in response, their leaders claimed, to the growing nationalist rhetoric of Croatia's politicians. Tensions were mounting everywhere. By December that year the relatively prosperous Republic of Slovenia voted overwhelmingly for independence from Yugoslavia. By the spring of 1991 there was fighting between Serb irregular forces and Croatian police units. In May 1991 Croatia voted for independence. On 25 June both Slovenia and Croatia declared independence. A ten-day war ensued in Slovenia as Yugoslav troops and tanks made a half-hearted attempt to keep the Republic within Yugoslavia. They failed.

The conflict in Croatia gained new momentum as the JNA (Yugoslav People's Army) was withdrawn from Slovenia and moved to Croatia. The fighting began in earnest. TV images of the Serb siege of Vukovar were beamed around the world and, for the first time, the international public was made aware of the scale of the conflict as Serb artillery gradually reduced the once-beautiful city to rubble. The historic coastal city of Dubrovnik was

also shelled. After months of fighting, Germany recognised the new inde-
pendent Croatia and, not long after, a UN Mission was sent in. The fighting
all but stopped. The relative quiet was deceptive; it was simply a precursor
to the nightmare that was about to unfold in Bosnia. In Sarajevo there was
still the mistaken belief that war could be avoided, that the multi-ethnic
population would not allow the city to descend into conflict.

Bosnia's General Election in 1990 had seen an overwhelming result in
favour of the three recently formed nationalist parties, representing the
three main ethnic groups. The parties formed what was, superficially, a
government of national unity led by Alija Izetbegović. But relations
between them soon deteriorated. On 27 February 1991 Izetbegović told
Parliament: 'I would sacrifice peace for a sovereign Bosnia-Herzegovina,
but for that peace in Bosnia-Herzegovina I would not sacrifice sover-
eignty.' In July 1991, while on a visit to Turkey, Izetbegović asked to join
the Organisation of Islamic Countries. This was hardly a crime but was
bound to provoke a hostile reaction from the other parties. By late-1991
people in military uniform began appearing on the streets. Yugoslav Army
convoys were seen moving around, some taking up positions on the hills
surrounding Sarajevo. Some people decided to leave the city.

Behind the scenes, Serb and Croat politicians were discussing between
themselves the division of Bosnia. Serbs started declaring 'Serb
Autonomous Areas'. And then on 14 October 1991 Radovan Karadžić
made his infamous speech in the Bosnian Parliament which appeared to
be a direct threat to the Muslims of Bosnia:

You want to take Bosnia-Herzegovina down the same highway of hell
and suffering that Slovenia and Croatia are travelling. Do not think
that you will not lead Bosnia-Herzegovina into hell, and do not
think that you will not perhaps make the Muslim people disappear,
because the Muslims cannot defend themselves if there is war – how
will you prevent everyone from being killed in Bosnia-Herzegovina?

The Parliamentary session was adjourned by the Serb speaker and the
Serb deputies walked out. The remaining Croat and Muslim deputies
voted in favour of Bosnian sovereignty. Ten days later the Serbs declared
their own parliament and voted to remain in Yugoslavia.

In December 1991 the European Community offered each of the six

Yugoslav republics recognition if they pledged to adopt the EC's criteria for the existence of new states. Izetbegović wanted Bosnia to be independent. The alternative, he argued, was being part of a greater Serbia.

But this was precisely what the Serbs did not want and Karadžić, believing that conflict was likely, went to Belgrade to request that all Bosnian Serbs serving in the JNA throughout Yugoslavia be transferred to Bosnia. In January 1992 Milošević issued a secret order to carry this out.

At the end of February Bosnians voted in a referendum on independence. Most Serbs boycotted it, anticipating the result. On 1 March there was a gangland-style attack on a Serb wedding party in the centre of Sarajevo. The groom's father-in-law was killed. Within hours Serb barricades were erected all around Sarajevo. To this day many Serbs argue that this shooting at the wedding was the real start of the Bosnian War. But the reality was different. Events had already gained a momentum of their own.

Meanwhile Karadžić himself balanced his increasingly busy political commitments with work at the main Kosevo Hospital in Sarajevo, in the Nedjo Zec psychiatric clinic. His political headquarters became the seventh floor of the Holiday Inn, opposite the Parliament building. According to one journalist,* 'Meeting him then was like preparing for an audience with a Mafia don. Young men with Kalashnikovs knocked on the door towards evening announcing that Dr Karadžić was ready to receive. In the Olympic suite, the boys in the anteroom frisked the visitors before entering, hanging around afterwards to bring the coffee which Karadžić sugared. A genial host, a nice guy with a sting in his tail, who was paranoid about his own security.' Karadžić also decided to move his family into the hotel, fearing they could be targeted if they remained in their old apartment in the centre of Sarajevo. On 27 March he become President of the National Security Council of the Serbian Republic.

Sarajevo was on a knife edge. But in eastern Bosnia things had already gone over the edge. The notorious Serbian paramilitary leader, Arkan, had led his forces into the Bosnian town of Bijeljina on 1 April. They targeted the non-Serb population and carried out summary executions. As news of the atrocities emerged, Izetbegović ordered a general mobilisation of the Bosnian territorial defence on 4 April. Karadžić was outraged: 'It was a great shock for us and we knew that this would lead to a war

* Maggie O'Kane writing in the *Guardian*, 10 August 1992.

... I said he should find some kind of formula to recall it [the mobili-sation order] because it was never too late. But he would not do it.'

On the same day, Serb irregulars surrounded the Sarajevo police academy on a hill above the city centre. As they did so, a peaceful demon-stration involving thousands of Sarajevans, protesting against the slide to war, was taking place outside the Parliament building. As the march proceeded in the direction of the police academy, Serb snipers fired into the crowd. A twenty-one-year-old medical student from Dubrovnik was killed. That night JNA tanks, under the cover of darkness and an artillery bombardment, seized control of Sarajevo airport.

On the afternoon of 6 April the European Union recognised Bosnia as an independent state. The United States followed suit the next day. Karadžić had warned that if independence were declared, it would not last a day. As he put it, the independent state would be 'still-born'. Immediately, he proclaimed the independent Serbian Republic of Bosnia and Herzegovina (later to be renamed Republika Srpska). The protests in Sarajevo continued outside the Holiday Inn. At one point, firing broke out and six protestors were killed. Bosnian militiamen stormed the hotel. A gunfight ensued. Six men were arrested and dragged off. But Karadžić had already left.

A general was holding an exhibition of his paintings in a gallery in the newly built Turkish cultural centre in Sarajevo. He spent most weekends in the countryside painting landscapes. There was free wine and canapés and you could buy one of his paint-ings – the cheapest was €250. At the bar, I chatted to the general-turned-artist. He told me there was one simple reason why Karadžić had not been arrested: the hard-line Serbs were just too loyal and would do anything to protect him. He said that in the past efforts to pursue the hunt had not been 'joined up' but this had now changed. He said the most likely way that Karadžić would be caught would be by chance or a lucky break.

By the end of the summer, the issue of Srebrenica resurfaced. The President of the Serb half of Bosnia, Dragan Čavić, went on television and came as close as was possible to making an apology. He said what had happened there in July 1995 was a 'black page in the history of the Serb people'. Those Serbs who had carried out the killings had committed a crime against their own people. Until now, Serb politicians had never acknowledged the scale of the atrocity nor the involvement of Serb forces. Ironically, Čavić was a member of the SDS, the party Radovan Karadžić had founded. His statement followed the publication of a report by the Bosnian Serb authorities. This report concluded that 'grave' violations of human rights had taken place and there had been a clear attempt to conceal evidence. It also revealed the discovery of 32 previously unknown mass graves.

It also now transpired that the issue of Srebrenica had been a central element to previously unreported negotiations aimed at securing the surrender of the former Bosnian Serb leader.

An article in one of Sarajevo's newspapers, quoting a former Prosecutor at the ICTY, revealed that Karadžić – or associates of Karadžić – had been in negotiations with The Hague as far back as 1999. I contacted the official and he confirmed to me that an approach had actually been made to The Hague as early as 1997. There were more contacts in 1998, then, in the following year, a series of meetings between intermediaries. It was suggested that if the charges regarding Srebrenica were dropped, the former President might be persuaded to give himself up. The Prosecutor told me there had been no question of dropping any charges and so the talks, such as they were, ended.

I made another trip to the Pink House. The family told me that Karadžić's mother, Jovanka, had broken her hip a couple of weeks earlier and they would be going to Montenegro for two weeks the next day. Jovanka was in hospital in Nikšić. They would see her and combine it with a holiday at the coast. Jovanka had had four heart attacks in five years. I decided it was finally time for me to visit the village where Karadžić had been born. If there was one thing I knew about him, it was that his roots and his family were central to everything he believed in. Also, the bleak, remote mountains of Montenegro offered a perfect place to hide.

8

Into the Mountains

'Wherever you go in the region, everyone has a tragedy
to relate, from whatever side they come. History is so
fresh in people's minds. One can't help but feel that the
pain must be passed down to the next generation. And
what does that mean for the future?' – Diary excerpt,
2 September 2004

My ancient jeep struggled along the narrow road. We could
see houses in the distance at the foot of the mountain. A
white-washed church stood sentinel on a raised piece of land
at the entrance to the village. The last stage of the journey
had been difficult and we were obliged to ask a number of
people for directions. Finally we had arrived in Petnica, the
village where Radovan Karadžić was born. How would we be
received? Was there a chance he might even be here?

It had been a long and tiring drive, following a winding,
roller-coaster road across southern Bosnia and northern
Montenegro in the hot August sun. Landslides and bad roads
had made the journey even more difficult. As we crossed into
Montenegro my fixer, Marko, burst out singing: *'Durmitor,
Durmitor, visoka planina . . .'* (Durmitor, Durmitor, high mountain . . .). We took a break at the Serbian monastery at Plužine
and looked down at the huge dam that dominated the valley,
providing hydro-electric power, a crucial resource for the local
economy.

Two sheer cliffs loomed over the town. I knew from the

map that one of them was called *Vojnik* or Soldier. Karadžić had spent his early years in the late-1940s in and around Šavnik. In those days, the town was rebuilding itself after the Second World War and perhaps there had been an air of optimism then. But today the place looked drab and depressing. A few buildings had been given a cursory lick of paint but there was more graffiti than there were bright colours. Rubbish was strewn on wasteland close to the centre and hunting dogs bayed in their kennels close to the shallow river which dribbled its way through town. We parked near a betting shop called Aristocrat.

It was lunchtime and we decided to look for something to eat before heading on to the village. The only establishment that looked as if it might serve food was the rundown Communist-era hotel overlooking the town. Every town in the former Yugoslavia had one of these places, usually empty shells. We opened the creaking door and entered the cavernous restaurant with its predictably empty tables and stained table-cloths. The solitary waiter – there was only ever one in places like this – was puffing on a cigarette in the far corner and listening to some screeching music on a fuzzy-screened TV. We stayed just long enough to take the edge off our hunger with a stale sandwich and a thick Turkish-style coffee to wash it down.

We set off again on the last leg of our journey. A growing sense of apprehension rose within me. We had no appoint-ment, we did not know who lived here (apart from possible members of the Karadžić family) and we were a long way from any major road, never mind any major town. Would there be a hostile reaction to our presence? Would people simply ignore us? Or would the village be empty? After all, it was the height of summer and many of the inhabitants, might be away. We passed a church then turned left on to a track and bumped down into Petnica. After a few hundred metres we spotted three men working in the garden of one of the houses. They stopped and stared at us. We pulled over. I asked Marko to try and break the ice.

He got out of the jeep and casually lit a cigarette. I remained in my seat, trying to look relaxed.

'Hi . . . how's it going?' he said. 'I wonder if you could help me. I am looking for the Karadžić family.'

There was a long pause.

'My name is Karadžić,' said one of the men.

'My name is Karadžić too,' said another.

'We are all Karadžićs here in this village,' came the response from the third man.

'Aha, I see, very good!' Marko laughed heartily, instantly shattering the atmosphere of menace that seemed to be building.

'Ha-ha! And I am Marko and I am a Serb. We have just driven from Pale in Bosnia,' he said engagingly. 'Pleased to meet you!'

One of the men smiled, and the other two visibly relaxed.

Whenever you travel to places in the Balkans, and especially when working as a journalist, you must choose very carefully who you take with you. While everyone denies having prejudices, being anti-this or anti-that, the truth of the matter is that one of the most evil legacies of the war is that people are automatically suspicious of those from other ethnic groups. Taking an Albanian interpreter into a Serb area of Kosovo, or vice versa, or a Serb interpreter to interview the victims of Srebrenica, or a Croat interpreter to Belgrade . . . all of these scenarios are likely to invite trouble. Choosing the right fixer or interpreter for a particular story is just as important as finding the right person to interview and the right questions to ask. In this case, Marko was the perfect person for the job.

Within a few short minutes we were invited to follow one of the men to what we understood to be his home. A short time later we parked outside what was clearly the oldest building in the village apart from the church. The man told us it was called Kula Karadžić (or Karadžić Tower). Its stone walls were at least three feet thick and it was pleasantly cool inside. On the walls hung pictures of Radovan Karadžić as well as Vuk Karadžić, the nineteenth-century Serbian writer who had done much to rationalise the Serbian language. There were also pictures of Ostrog Monastery and, more bizarrely, a picture of the old Communist-style hotel in Šavnik where we had just had lunch. I was offered *rakia* and coffee. We engaged in some light chat, and then I explained what I was doing there.

Our host suggested we should meet his cousin who was, apparently, an expert in Karadžić family history. He made a quick phone call and a few minutes later the cousin arrived, wearing blue overalls and carrying an axe. He introduced himself as Srdjan and explained that he had just been out chopping wood.

Srdjan was wearing large glasses and had the grey hair of a man in his fifties. He talked fast and gave the strong impression that he was less than delighted to see a foreign journalist in Petnica enquiring about Radovan Karadžić. But over a few more *rakias*, Marko worked his magic and Srdjan finally agreed to take us on a tour of the village.

There were no more than 20 houses. Our guide said that everyone in the village had the surname Karadžić. The family had lived here for centuries. We reached the small grey-stone church with its solitary bell and small cross perched on top of the roof. The only name inscribed on any of the gravestones was that of Karadžić. Apparently, the original foundations of the church dated back to the thirteenth century. Boldly, I asked Srdjan if he could take us to the actual place where the village's most famous son had been born. He shook his head, saying he could not do that without specific permission from members of the close family.

We were treated to an early-evening meal of pork and cheese and there was a never-ending supply of *rakia* and beer. I tried my best to keep up with the conversation but eventually decided to excuse myself from the table and went outside to call Sonja, to see whether she would give permission for us to visit the birthplace of her father. She told me that there would not be a problem and she would have a word with Srdjan. But she strongly advised me not to visit the house of Jovanka Karadžić, half an hour's drive away in Nikšić. There were a number of people there monitoring the building, sitting in jeeps outside. These, she said, were secret service agents waiting to see if Radovan would come to visit his ailing mother. So we agreed with Srdjan that he would escort us to the birthplace the next day.

I had arranged for us to do another interview in Montenegro with someone I had wanted to meet for a long time. He had been a close adviser to Karadžić during the war but soon afterwards had also disappeared off the radar screen. I had managed to track him down through a friend of a friend of a friend (the usual way in Bosnia) and he had agreed to meet me. These days he was living on the Montenegrin coast and it would take several long hours along tortuous roads to reach him.

The man's name was Jovan Zametica and he had been at the very heart of the Bosnian Serb leadership. Born in Banja Luka in Bosnia, his original name had been Omer Zametica, the son of a Bosnian Muslim father and a half-Serb mother. He had later moved to England, changed his name to John and then, finally, the Serbian Jovan. He was working as an academic in Britain when, in 1993, he decided to trade in his safe career to travel to Bosnia and offer his services to the Bosnian Serb leadership. The fact that he had been in England and spoke with an upper-class accent, had studied at Cambridge and apparently come from nowhere suddenly to be at the right hand of Karadžić, had prompted speculation at the time that he might have been working for British intelligence.

It was already dark when we reached his large house, a stone's throw from the sea, with its high wrought-iron gates. Zametica's accent really was cut-glass. He led us upstairs to his large living room. Small and bespectacled, he exuded the manner of an enthusiastic librarian. Thousands of books filled the floor-to-ceiling bookcases on one wall. Maps, historical pictures and cartoons covered the others.

I asked him how on earth he had ended up in Pale during the war. 'Well ... obviously I work for MI6,' he replied with a laugh before settling himself in his chair. Presumably this was a joke. As the conversation continued, he admitted he had not been looking forward to a lifetime career in academia and, through contacts, had seen his opportunity to, as he put it, 'make a difference'. He had headed to Bosnia and Pale in October 1993 to offer his insights into how the West might be planning to deal with the whole Bosnian issue. There he became close to Karadžić. Over the couple of hours we talked he told me Karadžić had been a very religious man; that the rumours he was a big gambler were false and had probably been spread by friends of Milošević in order to discredit him. He claimed Karadžić had had nothing to do with Srebrenica. He also claimed that he had been personally involved in setting up the deal with Holbrooke, that it was done but no document was ever signed. After that he would say no more. We left his house and decided to spend the night on the coast at a small pension.

The next day we retraced our route to Petnica. Srdjan had metamorphosed into a chatty guide, delighted to show us anything we wanted. His talk with Sonja had obviously had the desired effect. As the sun rose in the sky he took us for another walk, this time away from the village across the fields of apple and pear trees, cracking jokes along the way. I still remember one of them.

'During the Bosnian War some Serbs were carrying dead Muslims on their shoulders, wrapped up. They arrived at a UN checkpoint and the UN soldiers asked them what they were carrying. One of the Serbs replied, "Bears." The UN soldier said: "Grizzly?" (Which in Serbian means "bitten".) "No," says the Serb, "they are *Klali*."' (*Klali* means 'cut by the throat'.) Srdjan burst out laughing before I had even understood the punchline. When it was translated, I smiled politely and turned away.

Eventually we arrived at a grassy slope where he led us to a small tree surrounded by bushes. On closer examination I could see a few bricks and the remnants of a wall amidst the overgrown nettles and grasses. 'This is where he was born,' said Srdjan, and looked at us as if expecting exclamations of awe and wonder.

He saw my expression. 'Maybe great people are born from ashes,' he prompted me.

I took a few photos and by the time we had arrived back at the village it was already lunchtime. In the shade of Kula Karadžić we were again invited to share in meat and cheese and more *rakia*. Our conversation evolved into a history lesson about the region and the crucial role the Karadžićs had supposedly played in it. It reminded me again of just how important their history was to these people. Generation after generation had been raised on the heroic deeds of the past, battles fought and won against Ottoman or German, Italian or Partisan.

We spent the night at the ex-Communist hotel. It was cold, but there was nowhere else to stay. The next day we took a different route back to Sarajevo in order to witness a special Serbian nationalist celebration on the border between Serbia and Bosnia.

It was the 200th anniversary of the first Serbian uprising against the Turks in 1805. A two-day celebration was to culminate in the unveiling of a four-metre high bronze statue of the leader of the uprising, Karadjordje Petrović. The event took place on a hill above the Serbian monastery at Dobrun in southern Bosnia. We arrived late at night just as the celebrations were drawing to a close. The stalls selling Serbian nationalist emblems were still open, purveying amongst other things T-shirts printed with pictures of Karadžić, Mladić, and the hero of the Second World War, Draža Mihailović. In the main bar, as the beer flowed, a band was singing songs praising the heroic deeds of the former Bosnian Serb President. Another song was about Zoran Djindjic, the assassinated Serbian Prime Minister, and stated that the singer was not sorry that he was dead because he 'gave away too much', a reference to his willingness to co-operate with the UN War Crimes Tribunal.

We got talking to a man from Pale. He was full of praise for Karadžić. After a few drinks, I asked him where he thought Karadžić was now. He said he did not know but that he could tell me one thing: all of Karadžić's bodyguards from the war (and he named them) were now living in Pale, so whoever was protecting him now, it was not his old comrades-in-arms.

COUNTS 9 and 10
TERROR, UNLAWFUL ATTACKS

Radovan KARADŽIĆ, in concert with other members of this joint criminal enterprise, established and implemented, and/or used members of the [Serb] Sarajevo Forces to establish and implement a military strategy that used sniping and shelling to kill, maim, wound and terrorize the civilian inhabitants of Sarajevo. The sniping and shelling killed and wounded thousands of civilians of both sexes and all ages, including children and the elderly.

The ICTY indictment against Karadžić covers the three-and-a-half years of the Bosnian War. In summary, he is accused of genocide, crimes against humanity and violations of the laws and customs of war. The three main areas where these charges apply are the siege of Sarajevo; the setting up and running of brutal detention centres; and the massacre at Srebrenica. The phrases that occur again and again are the accusation that he acted 'individually or in concert with others' and 'knew or had reason to know that Bosnian Serb forces under his direction and control were committing the acts or had done so. And that he failed to take the necessary and reasonable measures to prevent such acts or punish the perpetrators thereof.'

The siege of Sarajevo was the longest in the history of modern warfare. It lasted more than three and a half years. More than 10,000 people, mainly civilians, were killed, and countless more injured. For much of that time the 400,000 citizens of the Bosnian capital were without basic necessities such as running water and electricity. Communication with the outside world was, at best, sporadic. A simple trip to find water or firewood in wintertime invited a game of Russian roulette with the snipers and mortar gunners on the hills surrounding Sarajevo.

The most notorious events were the two so-called market-place massacres in the centre of Sarajevo, on 5 February 1994 in which 68 civilians were killed, and on 28 August 1995 in which 37 people were killed. The second of these finally prompted massive NATO bombing raids on the Serb forces which ultimately led to the end of the war.

The psychological damage caused to the people of Sarajevo is still being assessed today. Karadžić and the Bosnian Serb leadership argued that it was never a siege but rather a defensive line set up to protect the 'Serb lands' and people living near Sarajevo. But this did not explain the indiscriminate shelling and shooting of thousands of civilians trapped in the city. In a very limited way, the siege was eventually broken when a small tunnel was built by the government under the airport, which linked their forces and provided a lifeline out of the city. Goods, medicines and soldiers passed in and out this way.

During 1992 Karadžić rapidly acquired a number of titles and positions at the top of the political and military hierarchy of the Serb-controlled territory in Bosnia. According to The Hague's indictment, on 27 March 1992 he became President of the National Security Council of Republika Srpska; on 12 May 1992 he became a member of the three-member Presidency of the Serbian Republic, and, on the same day, President of the Presidency; from 17 December 1992 he was sole President of the RS; and from 20 December 1992 he was Supreme Commander of the armed forces and presided over sessions of the Supreme Command. He held these positions until his resignation on 19 July 1996. On paper, at least, he was the most powerful and effective leader of the Bosnian Serbs. The only person who would ultimately challenge him in this role was his military commander General Ratko Mladić.

The siege of Sarajevo lasted from April 1992 until February 1996. The Bosnian Serbs made a half-hearted attempt to take the city right at the start of the conflict but their tanks were caught in the narrow streets and destroyed. From then on the Serbs would remain in the hills and on one side of the River Milacka, in the suburb called Grbavica. They spent much of the next few years shelling and sniping at buildings, civilians and military structures within the city. With superior weaponry and heavier artillery and guns, they were in a position to cause massive damage in the city below them. But they were always outnumbered in terms of infantry. The result was deadlock.

For most of the siege and during the war Karadžić lived in the family home in Pale. Much of his time was spent at the Presidency building, the former Hotel Panorama overlooking Pale. It was a family affair with his wife often by his side, especially when on foreign peace talks. His daughter Sonja was his chief press secretary. She was the key point of access for any journalists wishing to interview her father or to travel to report from different parts of Republika Srpska. Karadžić would often entertain foreign journalists, explaining the Serb position. He would show maps of how Bosnia should be divided up while sipping Cognac and smoking Cuban cigars. Just ten miles away, the shelling and shooting in Sarajevo would be taking place.

During the summer of 1992, he travelled to London as the former British Foreign Secretary, Lord Carrington, headed the European Community's efforts to broker a peace deal. Despite apparent break-throughs, and promises by all parties, events on the ground continued to spiral out of control.

At the end of 1992 the BBC produced a programme called 'Serbian Epic'. It followed Karadžić around and gave an insight into the thinking and personality of the Bosnian Serb leader. It showed him playing the single-stringed instrument, the gusle, *and visitng his mother in Montenegro. He was seen preparing for peace talks and rallying the troops. He was already becoming a war hero, a Serb legend. At one point, a Serb singer recites the following:*

> *Hey, Radovan, you man of steel!*
> *The greatest leader since Karadjordje!*
> *Defend our freedom and our faith*
> *On the shores of Lake Geneva.*

If he had been reluctant to take on the leadership of the Bosnian Serbs at the start of the war, any doubt had now disappeared. He was in charge. There was no going back.

The British General placed his hands together on the table and leaned towards me. 'At the end of the day, you must remember that it's the responsibility of the local authorities to arrest war crimes fugitives,' he said. It was the standard line used by all peacekeeping generals and politicians. It was partly true. After all, Bosnia was an independent country – as was

Serbia. They had the police and the intelligence services. But the reality was different and everyone knew it. At that time, the authorities did not have the will even though they probably had the means to track down Europe's most wanted men.

Major General David Leakey was commander of the new EU military force in Bosnia. At the end of 2004 the NATO force SFOR handed over most of its responsibilities, including the maintenance of a 'safe and secure' environment, to the European Union. The EU force, known as EUFOR, numbered around 7,000 troops and was deployed across the country. Bureaucrats in Brussels christened it Althea, after the Greek goddess of healing. Amongst its key supporting tasks, it was to provide support to the International Criminal Tribunal for the Former Yugoslavia (ICTY) and relevant authorities, including the detention of Persons Indicted for War Crimes (PIFWCs), and to support the fight against crime, not least by providing information and the security environment in which the police could act against the organised criminal networks. But NATO was not leaving town. A residual headquarters and a presence of a couple of hundred was committed to help promote reform of the Bosnian armed forces, collect intelligence, direct anti-terrorism and provide support for The Hague Tribunal. So there were now two international military organisations in the country dealing with war crimes. The commanders of both organisations denied that this was duplication. They said they had complementary capabilities, that they would support each other and it would be for the benefit of everyone.

I was interviewing General Leakey in his headquarters at Butmir on the outskirts of Sarajevo. It was November 2004.

'Of course, despite the responsibilities of the local authorities, if we got intelligence about the location of one of the war crimes fugitives, we would not miss the opportunity,' he told me.

In fact, Leakey seemed determined to make progress on the war crimes issue which was becoming an increasing embarrassment to the West. A few weeks after my interview with him, he did something that no one had done before. Using his far-reaching powers (and well-armed troops) he exposed one of the most secret and protected Bosnian Serb military facilities in the country. He claimed war crimes fugitives, including Ratko Mladić, had been hiding there. I was one of the few invited to visit the vast underground complex.

Our convoy plunged into the thick, snow-covered forest outside the town of Han Pijesak, an hour's drive from Sarajevo. The trees grew so dense and so close to the road that a premature darkness appeared to have descended. I saw a burned out, overturned car in a clearing. On the way there, I had seen old Yugoslav-era signs warning that photography was forbidden. At the end of the road we were now travelling along, far away from prying eyes, was the former wartime headquarters of the Bosnian Serb army which were tunnelled into a mountain. The darkness, the cold, the history, all created a powerful sense of foreboding. Our convoy comprised EUFOR peacekeeping jeeps and a few civilian cars. We were not expecting trouble but you never could tell.

We pulled up outside a single detached house. A sign announced that it was called the Villa Javor. A Rottweiler paced in a cage nearby. Behind the house, I noticed the heavily wooded ground sloping upwards. A couple of Bosnian Serb soldiers looked slightly bemused by our sudden arrival. Without any ceremony, General Leakey led us to the garage attached to the building. At the back was a low door made of steel twelve inches thick. The General lifted a heavy lever and we followed him down a wide corridor which led to another massively thick steel door. Beyond it was a whole complex of tunnels, meeting rooms, kitchens, bedrooms, map rooms and communications facilities. There was an air-filtration system, an underground water supply, and fuel-storage facilities. It was straight out of a James Bond movie. In one of the en-suite bedrooms, there was a large double bed with a tiger's head design on the bedspread. Someone mentioned this was where Mladić had been sleeping. 'This place can keep a hundred and fifty men for two weeks on full rations,' said our guide. But that looked like an underestimate to me.

'We know he's been here, so we now have this bunker under strict observation,' Leakey told me. Someone else claimed he had been here as recently as July, allegedly to spend time with his old wartime buddies, celebrating birthdays and going hunting.

Exposing the underground facility to public gaze was intended to step up the pressure on the fugitives. But the fact was that the trail, especially in the case of Karadžić, had been cold for a long time. This was confirmed to me by a high-level source whom I shall call 'Jonathan'. I had got to know him over a period of months, both socially and through work. We used to meet in an anonymous bar called Don near the football stadium of Zeljo, one of the two Sarajevo teams. It was always during the day when the place was fairly empty. In January 2005 he told me that the West had been in the dark about Karadžić since 1997. 'He could be in Kazakhstan, as far as we are aware,' he said. 'The peacekeepers, the spy agencies, The Hague ... they don't have a clue. As far as I am aware the most recent photograph of him is a decade old. He could look like anything now.' He also told me that some of the people looking for Karadžić had been corrupted by money and that the leaking of information had hindered the hunt. Despite the efforts of the EUFOR commander and others, Karadžić still seemed a long way from being captured.

On a dark and windy night in Sarajevo, I was having dinner in a Thai restaurant with another spy. He had short hair and glasses. He laughed easily, apparently without inhibition. When the talk became more serious, his eyes hardened and a steely note came into his voice. When the talk turned to skiing and other innocuous subjects, his shoulders would relax and his eyes would soften. The speed with which he could switch from one manner to the other unnerved me. I was simply not sure what to believe. Was it all the truth or were there some stories intended to misdirect me?

'You know, we could write an obituary together announcing that Karadžić has died,' he suggested. 'We could do it for one of the major newspapers.' He picked up his glass of red wine, cocking his head to one side to consider my reaction to his idea.

'Why? What would be the point?' I asked.

'Well, we know what type of person he is. There's a chance he would respond. Either he or his supporters could write in to deny that he was dead, possibly even offering proof that he was alive. If he or they did that, we might be able to trace where their response came from, and from there we might be able to find him.'

'Yes,' I said, totally unconvinced by the idea but intrigued by its audacity. 'Let me think about it,' I lied.

Over our four-hour dinner, the man admitted that Western governments had new priorities in Bosnia. It was not all about tracking down and arresting war criminals who had been on the run for years. Nowadays, the key priority was dealing with the threat of Islamic terrorism.

'Let us be honest,' he said, carefully placing his glass of wine on the table. 'Apprehending Karadžić is important, especially from a moral point of view. But the priority, the number one interest of my government, is terrorism and the threat to my country. Karadžić does not pose a threat to my country. Terrorists do.'

But I had my own agenda.

'Do you know where Karadžić is? Or how to find him?' I asked.

'If you want to hide, you hide in a city. That is where you do it, it is the best place. You want to be somewhere you can be anonymous. That's safest. You should look for him in Belgrade,' he said with the confidence of someone who just might know. And there was more.

'If Belgrade wants to arrest Karadžić, or Mladić for that matter, they can do it. This is not an intelligence-led operation now. This is about politics, about using political pressure to force the arrest. If he is in a foreign country, what can we do?

We do not have the power to go and kidnap him and send him to The Hague. We rely on the co-operation of the local authorities.'

As I wandered home past the Ali Pasina mosque later that night, I reflected on my conversation with the spy. There had been the suspicion for a long time that war crimes fugitives had found a safe haven in Serbia and, particularly, Belgrade. Now there was growing evidence that this was indeed the case. In October 2004 the house of Ljubisa Beara was surrounded by Serbian police and he was given an ultimatum: he should either surrender voluntarily or be unceremoniously arrested.

Beara had been Mladić's intelligence chief and had been indicted for genocide for his role at Srebrenica. Up until this point the Serbian Government, led by Vojislav Koštunica, had stuck to the line that it would only encourage indictees to surrender voluntarily to The Hague. At the time this policy was still adhered to officially. The fact that Beara's house had been surrounded and he had been given an ultimatum was not publicised. But from that moment on it became clear to other indictees that the writing was on the wall. Over the coming months, nearly 20 fugitives made the trip to The Hague. The accused were offered guarantees by the Serbian Government so they could be released on bail. Financial support, amounting to €200 (£135) a month, was offered to them and their families, as well as air tickets and spending money for trips to The Hague. But why had there been this unannounced change in policy?

During the previous 12 months, the United States had withheld $100 million worth of loans to Serbia. Peacekeepers in Bosnia had raided and closed down Bosnian Serb military bases. The chief international envoy to Bosnia, Lord Ashdown, had used his wide-ranging powers to sack dozens of politicians and policemen allegedly protecting war crimes suspects. Most recently, Croatia's bid to join the EU had been blocked for its failure to co-operate fully with the Tribunal. There had also been the political calculation that such arrests or 'persuasion' would not result in mass demonstrations in the streets of Belgrade. The fact was – and it was proved by the relatively peaceful way all these transfers occurred – that the vast majority of Serbs were weary of all the nationalistic talk when their economy was moribund and Serbia remained, to all intents and purposes, outside the international family of nations with no prospect of joining the European Union. The less important fugitives had been handed over, so would Karadžić and Mladić be next?

In October 2004 Karadžić had demonstrated his ability to thumb his nose at the West. His latest book was published. Entitled *Under the Left Breast of the Century*, it was a collection of poems, some of which were said to have been written during the past few months. One of the chapters was entitled 'I Can Look for Myself'. The book was launched in Požarevac, the home town of former Yugoslav President Slobodan Milošević, currently standing trial for war crimes in The Hague. Florence Hartmann, spokeswoman for Carla Del Ponte, said, 'It is outrageous that a fugitive and an indictee is free to write and have books published.'

Events now took a dramatic turn. Radovan Karadžić's mother, Jovanka, died in her home town in Montenegro. It was widely known that Radovan had been very close to her. The big question was whether he would finally take a risk and come out of hiding in order to attend her funeral. I knew I had to be there.

9

In the Shadow of the Church

'We are here to bury the honourable mother and wife from the honourable Montenegrin house of Karadžić. She was the mother of an immortal' – Metropolitan Amfilohije Radović, Head of the Serbian Orthodox Church in Montenegro, 7 May 2005

Montenegro is a land of extremes. Russian tycoons race their Ferraris and top-of-the-range Mercedes through the streets of its capital while peasants walk their horses on dirt tracks. Brutal snow-capped mountains dominate the interior while gentle winds fan Montenegro's Adriatic coastline with its clear blue waters. The country's history is a tale of war and invasion and resistance. You are the closest of friends or the deadliest of enemies; there is not much in between. The Church has always played a central role in the history of Montenegro, its priests never averse to dabbling in politics and warfare when the time was right. The 'warrior priests' of Montenegro date from at least the age of Prince-Bishop Petar II Petrović-Njegoš, author of the famous Serbian epic poem, 'The 'Mountain Wreath'. For some, Njegoš was the defender of the faith and the Serbian people; for others he was the father figure of a virulent brand of Serbian nationalism. So many truths. The occasion of the funeral of Jovanka Karadžić brought all these traditions together.

Once again I made the long trek south from Sarajevo, across the mountains and into Montenegro. Along the way I noticed the supposedly 'undercover' peacekeeper vehicles with their occupants studiously examining maps or eating sandwiches, eyes instantly flickering towards the road to check any passing car. As I approached the border crossing my mobile phone suddenly beeped. It was a text from my friendly spy. 'How is it going? Have you seen Radovan yet?' I sent a jokey reply and switched my phone off.

I had been on the move a lot recently, travelling between Bosnia, Serbia and Croatia. I had just attended a commemoration service at Jasenovac in Croatia where during the Second World War thousands of people, mainly Serbs, had been systematically butchered in a concentration camp run by Croatian Ustasha. I had interviewed the Croatian Prime Minister, Ivo Sanader, who was dealing with his own war crimes issue. The Hague had indicted Ante Gotovina who had been one of Croatia's top generals. He was a hero to many, but the Prosecutors had accused him of war crimes against Serbs. It was a difficult issue for the Croatian Government. In the shadow of the huge monument to the Serbian dead, Sanader finally clarified his position in his interview with me by saying he would arrest him. This was not the policy of the Serbian Prime Minister, Vojislav Koštunica.

He had made clear his reluctance to arrest fugitives, especially Karadžić and Mladić. I had just returned from Belgrade, having been promised an interview with him but, after I had waited around for two days, the appointment was cancelled. Instead, I interviewed the Minister for Co-operation with The Hague, Rasim Ljajić. 'The Hague Tribunal issue was certainly the most important obstacle to the process of Serbia and Montenegro's integration into the European and Euro-Atlantic institutions,' he told me. 'Every talk with the representatives of the international community starts and ends with the same topic – The Hague Tribunal. There was a huge distrust by the Hague towards us.' He insisted Serbia was doing all it could to locate fugitives and have them transferred to The Hague. A few days later, another general voluntarily surrendered to the authorities.

*   *   *

I arrived in Nikšić in the late-morning. The town, with its low-rise buildings and cracked pavements, had seen better days, but the tree-lined streets and pedestrian areas with their bars and cafes were attractive in their own way. The church in the centre, set on a little hill and surrounded by parkland, was postcard picturesque.

People had gathered in the churchyard under the branches of the old trees, the spring sunshine bathing building and people alike in its cleansing glow. Priests and undercover agents mingled with the mourners who huddled together in groups, exchanging hushed conversation and knowing glances. Many wore sunglasses, hiding their tears or their thoughts. Inside, Jovanka's open coffin lay on its podium. The incense from the priest's thurible swirled above her face before drifting away towards the congregation.

Members of the family, including her son Luka, with bald head and bushy white moustache, gathered around the coffin. They held candles as the sermon was delivered, listening intently to the words of the priest. But my attention was on the hard men in the congregation with suspicion etched into their leathery faces. Dressed in crumpled shirts and old jeans, they were keeping an eye open for any people who did not fit, did not belong at this most private of occasions. Not surprisingly, they seemed to be staring at me. Smartly dressed in jacket and tie, it was clear I was a reporter. I wandered slowly around the church, alternately taking photographs and recording the sound for radio.

Metropolitan Amfilohije, head of the Serbian Orthodox Church in Montenegro, imposing in black robes and long grey beard, gave a sermon praising Jovanka, comparing her to the mothers of past Serbian heroes. The primate had always been close to the family, especially during the hard times. He was also related to the Serbian Prime Minister, Vojislav Koštunica. His eyes were deep-set, making them difficult to read, but there was a twinkle in them as if he knew some absolute truth that no one else was privy to.

'We are here to bury the honourable mother and wife from the honourable Montenegrin house of Karadžić,' intoned

Amfilohije. 'She is the mother of an immortal. She told me once that she would prefer him to be brought back dead but faithful to his people and faith, rather than alive and a traitor to his people.'

I followed the coffin and mourners out of the church towards the plot where the interment would take place. I saw Ljiljana and Sonja, both dressed in black, Ljiljana wearing large black sunglasses. Amidst the flow of mourners, our paths crossed and I expressed my condolences.

I walked into the graveyard and watched as hundreds gathered around the hole in the ground where Jovanka Karadžić would be finally laid to rest next to her husband. Journalists clambered over the soil piled next to the grave. I stayed in the background and scanned the faces, looking for the man everyone wanted to see. But there was no sign. I saw priests and peasants, dark-suited men and extravagantly dressed women, cameras snapping and videos whirring. One man was not filming the coffin – his lens was focused on me. I trained my own video camera in his direction, using the zoom to focus in more closely. He was middle-aged with grey hair, I saw, before he quickly disappeared into the crowd.

Luka made a speech but I was too far away to hear. The priests carried out their final obsequies. The coffin was lowered into the earth and soil shovelled on top of it. The flowers piled around the grave reached head-height. A lone voice suddenly shouted, 'Long live Radovan!' The unacknowledged pressure and tension filling the air were suddenly released.

As I left the cemetery, I passed the board where the death notices were displayed. Underneath Jovanka's name and photograph were condolence messages from her children and grandchildren. The first name on the list was 'Radovan'.

Back in Sarajevo, I had another meeting with my contact Jonathan, at our usual rendezvous. 'Every day I'm less and less optimistic that we are ever going to find him,' he told me, sipping a late afternoon beer. 'Ninety-nine per cent of "information" that's received by the organisations involved in the hunt is just rubbish. NATO has its intelligence units, The Hague has its "tracking team", individual countries have their own agencies ... but the truth is, nothing is really achieved by all this effort. One of the problems is members of the public are trying to earn a quick buck by passing on information which turns out to be false. You know, they'll say, "I've got a nice bit of information but give me a hundred Euros first." Sometimes you do, sometimes you don't. But it's always a waste of time.'

When Karadžić disappeared in the winter of 1997–8, Slobodan Milošević was still in power. History shows that he and Karadžić had not been the closest of friends from about 1993–4. Milošević's sponsorship of the Bosnian Serb leader had been strong at the start of the Bosnian War but lessened as he began to realise that an early peace was the best way to ensure his own survival. He would not risk his own future to protect Karadžić. On the other hand, Karadžić's connections to the Church were long-standing and deep. His daughter had been baptised at the famous Ostrog Monastery and he had done a great deal for the Church during the war. In fact, Serbia's Church and state had been closely linked for generations. During the war some Serb priests were photographed carrying machine-guns or blessing paramilitaries before they went to the front line. They were not short of money either. Could the Serbian Orthodox Church be protecting the former President?

Back in Sarajevo, working through a pile of old newspaper cuttings, I established the fact that one of Karadžić's last public appearances, before he resigned his party and presidential positions, had been at the annual pilgrimage to Ostrog Monastery, close to his birthplace. The monastery, built into a mountain rock face, was founded by Sveti Vasilije (Saint Basil) in the seventeenth century. His tomb, in the chapel, had become a site of pilgrimage after reports of miracles occurring through the intercession of the saint. On 11 May 1996 Karadžić had attended the all-night annual pilgrimage. I determined now that I would attend the same ceremony. There was a very remote chance that my quarry would be there but, at the very least, I would gain an insight into the workings of the Church, and observe the building Karadžić had known well. I put the date in my diary: 11 May 2005.

The road there is steep and winding. Coaches sometimes have trouble negotiating the tight bends. But the view from the monastery to the valley below is quite breathtaking.

At this time of year local people set up stalls selling food, drink and religious paraphernalia. Music blares from cheap ghetto blasters. At some of the stalls you can buy pictures, T-shirts and key rings printed with photographs of Karadžić and Mladić.

I had arranged to visit the monastery via a Church contact in Belgrade. Now I introduced myself to a monk, explaining that I had heard a lot about the Sveti Vasilije festival and was hoping to meet the Metropolitan himself.

I was politely shown to a cool terrace area and asked to wait. A few minutes later vanilla ice cream and coffee were served. I relaxed in the shade as the occasional wasp flew sorties over the dregs of my melted ice cream. After a while I was shown into a meeting room where a number of local dignitaries were sitting on armchairs and sofas. The Vladika – or bishop – was presiding. Nuns served us all *rakia*, marshmallows, coffee and orange juice.

As the afternoon passed the talk meandered, covering everything from the dangers of religious fundamentalism to the amount of money that Chelsea football club now had to spend on new players since they had acquired a new Russian owner. We were all given Easter eggs as presents.

After the local dignitaries took their leave, I was invited to share dinner with the monks. In a hall in one of the buildings there was a long table with about 15 people sitting to either side of it. I took a place at one of the benches. We ate in silence. The only sound was the scraping of cutlery on metal plates: vegetable soup, roast potatoes, tuna, olives, an apple and fruit juice. After twenty minutes a bell rang. Everyone stood up and a prayer was said. Supper was over.

* * *

The central religious ceremony was to be held at midnight, higher up the mountain in the main part of the monastery, a white-washed edifice that had been built into the rock face. Thousands of other pilgrims made the same trek, many carrying sleeping bags and tents, all hoping to get close to the chapel where the remains of Sveti Vasilije rested.

A monk guided us past the queues, up winding staircases and narrow corridors, until finally we came to a small chapel, no larger than ten square metres, literally carved out of the rock. This was where the second of the three special liturgies was to take place. The air was thick with incense. Ancient frescoes decorated the rough-hewn walls. There were four priests and the same number of choir boys. The chapel could take no more. When the singing began, shivers ran down my spine. It was truly beautiful. I felt almost lost in time among these monks in their traditional habits, the precious icons and ancient music, all encompassed womb-like in the sheltering rock.

As we descended the hill in the early hours of the morning, pilgrims were still streaming their way upward. A few times I thought I spotted someone who might be Karadžić but every time I turned out to be mistaken. I spent the night in a dormitory owned by the monastery where the more privileged pilgrims paid a small fee for the luxury of a bed and a roof. I had been promised an audience with the Metropolitan the next day. Through the shutters of the dormitory I could see torchlight twinkling among the branches as the pilgrims continued their all-night vigil.

Morning dawned bright and sunny. I was introduced to a young priest in one of the coffee shops near the stalls, but our cheerful badinage did not last long. 'The Hague is a Serb prison,' he said. 'In Serbia we welcome all people from abroad. But Serbs are not welcome anywhere else.' He asked me if I wanted to hear a joke. I nodded. 'Slobodan Milošević's friend asked the President if he would do him a favour and buy him a luxury four-bedroomed house in the smartest area of Belgrade. The President said he would. The friend then asked him for a Ferrari. The President said OK. He then asked for a private jet. But Milošević said that was too much, he did not have enough money. "But you must have enough money," said the friend. "You have just sold Kosovo."'

Eventually, Metropolitan Amfilohije arrived with a small entourage of priests and monks. A few minutes later I was ushered into a room upstairs. It was dominated by a long table with green 1970s-style foam-filled chairs and sofas arranged on either side.

There were around a dozen other people there, including a senior policeman. A group of nuns served *rakia*. Amfilohije sat at the head of the table, a ceremonial stick in his right hand. He was smaller and slighter than I had thought, after seeing him at Jovanka's funeral. But there was no mistaking those deep-set eyes with their characteristic twinkle, and the respect with which everyone treated him. He started by saying that he did not want to talk about politics, and then proceeded to not only talk about politics but also to give me a historical and political lesson dating back to the fourth century.

Although Amfilohije spoke a number of languages, English was not one of them and my Serbian was still not good enough. His interpretation of the last sixteen hundred years thus had to be translated laboriously by a monk-interpreter. So I heard the history of Ostrog Monastery during the Second World War and an account of the fierce fighting that had taken place in the area. He said more than 20 soldiers of the Yugoslav Army were killed by the Partisans locally and their bodies thrown into a pit nearby. It was only in the last year that they were buried properly.

On the issue of whether Montenegro should be independent or not, he said it was ironic that, in a world which was coming together in forms like the European Union, some people still wanted to divide Montenegro and Serbia. Serbia and Montenegro, which were the only two Republics left after the collapse of Yugoslavia, formalised their relationship and called themselves the Union of Serbia and Montenegro in 2003. (This Union came to end in 2006 and both became independent, sovereign states.) Finally, he concluded with the gnomic phrase: 'The Church cannot live without Crucifixion.'

The public nature of the interview made it impossible for me to ask him any probing questions, but I calculated that establishing an amicable first meeting would be useful in the long term.

Back in Sarajevo I was handed a manila envelope containing a number of letters sent by Karadžić to his family. One of them had even found its way into a small newspaper in Montenegro. I had asked a contact to find out whether I could see these letters. Now I had them. They were photocopies of the originals, all signed by Radovan's hand. They were written in Serbian but, very handily, my contact had also managed to provide me with English translations. The letters dated from April 2001 to December 2002 and covered a whole range of subjects. He referred to the clothes that his family had been sending during his time on the run and discussed arranging more secret meetings with them. There were also instructions about the family businesses, selling the radio station, buying a flat in Pale. He commented on current political events and referred affectionately to his wife. It was a very personal insight into the world of Karadžić on the run.

The information was so detailed that there seemed to be numerous potential leads for tracking him down. This, I believed, was a huge breakthrough. My source was impeccable – someone working for an international security organisation in Bosnia – and so I wrote the story. It appeared prominently in a major newspaper. But, afterwards, there was silence. None of the organisations involved in hunting Karadžić seemed to take the letters seriously. The potential leads were not pursued. I asked my other contacts in the security world why they were not following up on the letters. I was met with blank stares. I asked if the letters were genuine. More blank stares and silence. Gradually, I realised that I had almost certainly been set up, that the letters were pure fiction and that I had simply been used. Someone was using me to try to get to Karadžić.

The entrance to the secret underground Bosnian Serb army base at Han Pijesak. Ratko Mladić was believed to have stayed here.

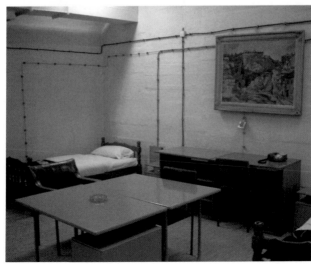

One of the bedrooms in the underground base at Han Pijesak. The facilities included map rooms, kitchens, meeting rooms and an underground water supply.

Serbian Prime Minister, Vojislav Kostunica, a nationalist who strongly opposed The Hague Tribunal. The author is in the bottom right of the picture. (AFP/Getty Images)

Vladimir Naždin, a former senior official in the Milošević government, claims to have seen the alleged deal between Karadžić and Richard Holbrooke.

Author at the huge Kosovo Rally outside the Federal Parliament in Belgrade, 21 February 2008. Later on, some of the demonstrators stormed the US Embassy.

The road where Karadžić was arrested, close to the blue police checkpoint on the outskirts of Belgrade.

Papers in Sarajevo announcing that Karadžić has been found.
'Karadžić Uhapsen' ('Karadžić Arrested') says *Dnevni Avaz* the country's
biggest-selling newspaper.

Special War Crimes Court, Belgrade, where Karadžić was taken a few days after his arrest.

Vladimir Vukčević, Serbia's Chief War Crimes Prosecutor.

The alternative health diploma that Karadžić received.

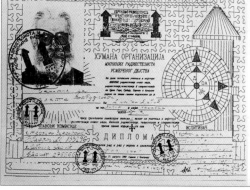

(*Above*) Business cards used by Karadžić under his assumed name of Dragan Dabić.
(*Below*) The building on the right in Yuri Gagarin Street, New Belgrade, was the last place Karadžić lived before he was caught. His flat was on the third floor.

Karadžić with Mina Minić, the man who taught him bio-energy techniques.
(AFP/Getty Images)

Radovan Karadžić appears in court in The Hague shorn of his beard. (Getty Images)

COUNTS 7 and 8
(DEPORTATION, INHUMANE ACTS)

Radovan KARADŽIĆ participated in a joint criminal enterprise to permanently remove Bosnian Muslims and Bosnian Croats from the territories of BiH claimed as Bosnian Serb territory by means which included the crimes of forcible transfer and deportation ... Beginning in March 1992, restrictive and discriminatory measures, arbitrary arrest and detention, harassment, torture, rape and other acts of sexual violence, killing, and destruction of houses and cultural monuments and sacred sites, all targeting Bosnian Muslims and Bosnian Croats in the Municipalities, as well as the threat of further such acts, caused Bosnian Muslims and Bosnian Croats to flee in fear. Others were physically driven out.

With the failure of more peace talks in London, another attempt at ending the bloodshed had been lost. As 1993 dawned, a new peace plan was put into motion, this time headed by two international negotiators: Lord Owen, former British Foreign Secretary, representing the EU, and Cyrus Vance, former US Secretary of State, representing the UN. Over the coming months the leaders of the warring parties would travel to and fro, between the Balkans, Geneva and New York, and the two negotiators and their teams would try to find a way of resolving the conflict.

On the ground, Bosnian Serb forces continued to consolidate their grip on the country, eventually controlling around 70 per cent of the territory. And the hard-liners had no intention whatsoever of making any concessions, even though Serbs only made up around 30 per cent of the population before the war. Much of their land grab had been won through mass intimidation and murder of the non-Serb population. This policy of 'ethnic cleansing', as it became known, was carried out by Serb troops, paramilitaries and irregulars, from Bosnia and from Serbia itself.

It is estimated that around 2,000,000 people, half of the entire population, would ultimately be displaced by the war. The vast majority of these people were Bosnian Muslims, but Croats and Serbs were also forced to flee. Ethnic cleansing was not a practice carried out by just one of the ethnic groups. But there was a clear plan by the Serb side to clear large swathes of land of the non-Serb population in eastern Bosnia, close to the border with Serbia and northern Bosnia. Journalists meeting Karadžić during the war described how he was continually looking at maps, trying to work out ways of dividing the country into three distinct regions for its three peoples. At times he used Switzerland or Belgium as models for a future Bosnia.

For those non-Serbs who did not choose to move from their villages or towns – or were just too slow in doing so – their fate was death or detention camp. Rumours of the existence of these camps had filtered down to journalists working in Sarajevo in the summer of 1992. There were tales of random executions, torture and starvation. Under pressure from journalists, Karadžić invited them to see the camps for themselves. The reports that came out afterwards shocked the world. Pictures of emaciated men standing behind barbed wire, their eyes full of fear, were reminiscent of the Nazi concentration camps of the 1940s.

Why Karadžić allowed the Western media to visit the camps in the first place remains a mystery. Maybe he thought the camps would have been sanitised before the journalists arrived, or maybe he did not know the true scale of the abuse. 'I did not receive regular reports about the prisons. Other people were in charge,' he said later. 'The police and Department of Justice are in charge of investigating them. I'm Head of State. When somebody tells me something is wrong, I send an order to investigate. I didn't even know about the prison in Omarska. I invited people to come and see for themselves in every corner of the country, opened camps to every humanitarian institution. There may be bad conditions in some prisons, but I didn't try to hide it.'

Allegations were also emerging of systematic rape carried out by Serb soldiers and paramilitaries. Some reports even referred to the existence of 'rape camps'. I met one woman who told me her story. She came from the northern Bosnian town of Prijedor:

On 24 July men with balaclavas came to the house where we were staying. They viciously beat my husband in front of the children and me. His head was bleeding. They tied his hands with wire and took him away. A few days later I saw him again for the last time. It was in the prison camp they had set up. He was shot dead in

*front of me, along with dozens of others. His blood sprayed on to
my clothes.*

*I was taken to the house outside the camp and kept there. One
night, the camp commander came to me. My two daughters were in
the bedroom sleeping. He used a knife to strip me. I fought back.
He stabbed me and then raped me. It was just the first time. It
happened this way, night after night, week after week. I told myself
I would survive. He said he wanted me to survive because it would
be more painful for me than dying. He was my former headmaster.*

*An insight into Karadžić's odd behaviour at the time was given by his
former deputy, Biljana Plavšić. Jailed for 11 years by The Hague Tribunal
for her role in the war, she produced a memoir entitled* I Testify.

*'The continuous picking of his ears with a pencil, spreading dandruff
from his hair, biting his nails until they bled and his changing day to
night, was drawing more and more attention from people,' she wrote.*

*He was often late for meetings. 'Presidency meetings were supposed
to be held every day at 11 a.m. Everybody was on time, except the
President . . . who was regularly late between one and two hours,' she
states. Dr Karadžić's wife used to cover for his absence. 'On two or
three occasions, I personally called his house and his wife always gave
the same, short answer, "Radovan is sleeping," and then she would
just hang up.'*

*She also claims Karadžić profited from the war: 'His ideal model of
a good leader is a profiteer who, in an irregular way, gets rich overnight;
the type of person who does not respect the law and rules, and uses war
and the tragedy of his people to smuggle humanitarian aid and becomes
a millionaire within two or three months. He was fascinated by those
people. He admired them, he hung out with them and he followed in their
footsteps.'*

*'There was always money for Karadžić's pockets . . . sometimes I
wondered if he was at all aware of what was going on, that people were
dying,' she records.*

And so the war dragged on.

Radovan Karadžić's son, Aleksandar or 'Sasa', was arrested by
SFOR troops in Pale on 7 July 2005. Members of the family

had been questioned before but they had never been arrested and taken away in such a dramatic fashion. New tactics were being employed by the peacekeepers.

Witnesses said Sasa was led away in handcuffs and a flak jacket, with a hood pulled over his head. He was held for ten days. In a statement, SFOR said the arrest was carried out because Sasa was suspected of giving support to his father and that he 'may have information vital to the goal of locating indicted war criminals or identifying their supporters.'

While Sasa was being questioned at an undisclosed location in Bosnia – although it was an open secret that detainees were questioned by the Americans at Eagle base in Tuzla – an important event was taking place in another part of the country. It was the tenth anniversary of the Srebrenica massacre. Lord Ashdown issued a statement:

> The worst crime to take place in Europe in the latter part of the twentieth century took place here. The world's failure to protect the people of this country and the people here in particular is our greatest shame. Most importantly, we must ensure that those responsible, Radovan Karadžić and Ratko Mladić, face justice in The Hague. In this way we will ensure that the truth of these terrible events is known and recognised. Serbia is moving from denial to recognition of the crimes that were committed here in their name. The way to absolve collective guilt is to establish individual guilt under the law. These crimes are the crimes of individuals and with the arrest and trial of those individuals we can start to say we are moving towards reconciliation.

The media circus came to town and so did a bunch of VIPs including the President of Serbia, Boris Tadić, the first time such a senior Serbian official had made the trip. Former US negotiator Richard Holbrooke also came and I managed to secure a brief interview with him. In response to my question about a deal with Karadžić, he replied:

That is, as I keep saying, C-R-A-P ... crap. It is something that Mr Karadžić put out in order to cover his massive humiliation at being forced to give up his two titles, President of Srpska and President of his party. So he put this lie out, and because he hasn't been captured some people still believe it. But it isn't true.

A few days later Sasa was released and returned to his family. Someone involved in the arrest operation later told me that they had taken 'real risks'. It was not made clear to me at the time what was meant by 'real risks' but I presumed it referred to the legality of the operation. And perhaps as a result, Ljiljana Karadžić rang a local journalist and said she would like to make a statement. Before the television cameras, she made this dramatic appeal:

> This is a message to my husband, Radovan Karadžić. I have to address you this way, because there is no other way. Our family is under constant pressure from all sides. We are being threatened in every way, our lives and our property. We are living in a constant atmosphere of concern, pain and suffering. That is why, between loyalty to you and loyalty to our children and grandchildren, I had to choose and I have chosen. I find it painful and hard to ask you, but I beg you with all my heart and soul to surrender. That will be a sacrifice for us, for our family. In the hope that you are alive and that you are free to make the decision yourself, I beg you to make the decision and do it for all our sakes. In all my helplessness and my weakness, the only thing that I can do is beg you.

For a few days I remained in Sarajevo waiting to see if Karadžić would respond to his wife's appeal. But nothing happened.

About this time, I arranged another interview with the General in charge of the EUFOR peacekeepers, David Leakey. EUFOR had been operating for six months and I wanted to know how they were progressing. I visited the military camp at Butmir where the NATO and EUFOR headquarters were co-located.

'Karadžić is hiding under a stone and I think that's disgraceful for somebody who was a leader of his people. Many of his subordinates are in The Hague and he should be there mitigating for them. If he was a proper leader, he'd be standing up for his convictions and he'd be defending himself and his people in court,' Leakey told me.

'Do you know where he is?' I asked.

'I never give any information about where people are. If I gave you any indication of how close we were to knowing where he was, then that would help him and I'm not going to do that in public.'

'It appears that the intelligence is just not good enough to find him. Is that right?'

'I think that if Radovan Karadžić chose to live in Bosnia-Herzegovina and was here on a regular basis ... our intelligence would be good enough to get him. He knows that and that's why his visits here are extremely secretive, extremely well planned, extremely fleeting and, possibly, extremely rare. But I don't want to give any more indications than that.'

There seemed to be the strong implication there that Karadžić was not in Bosnia. But Leakey's face remained impassive.

'If he was in neighbouring Montenegro or Serbia, what would you do?' I asked

'Well, I can't operate outside the boundaries of Bosnia-Herzegovina.'

'But you could send Special Forces in?'

'EUFOR cannot do that. Absolutely not, under any circumstances.'

'But it would be tempting?'

'Don't tempt me. I'm un-temptable. I'm incorruptible.' He smiled.

'Would you like to see more co-operation with neighbouring countries?'

'Increasingly, the co-operation is positive and the international community is becoming much more confident in the authorities in Serbia and Montenegro. But they have to deliver, not just talk a good talk.'

So much for the view from the military side.

I'd arranged to meet one of the region's most respected investigative journalists in the restaurant Cappuccino, on the banks of the river in Sarajevo. He had been following the Karadžić case for longer than I had. While devouring countless bowls of ice cream, he outlined what he knew – or at least what he was prepared to tell me.

A three-day meeting had recently taken place in Montenegro, he told me, involving representatives of intelligence agencies from the United States, Serbia, Montenegro and Bosnia. Karadžić was said to be staying at a monastery nearby. The former Bosnian Serb leader was apparently flitting between this monastery and an annex of Ostrog. The main intelligence agencies knew where he was but showed no interest in having him caught. Karadžić had protection on three levels: from the Church, a group of his own bodyguards and the secret police.

Was my informant merely speculating here or did he have proof that he did not want to share? As he finished his last bowl of ice cream, he raised his spoon. 'Watch out for the secret police in Montenegro. They can be quite unscrupulous,' he warned me.

That evening a friend came round to my flat. He had fought during the war, done his bit, and then, disillusioned like so many others, had found a passage out of Bosnia. And, like so many others, ended up a refugee travelling aimlessly around Europe. When he eventually returned he found a job with an international organisation. But he knew it would not last for ever and, anyway, he had other plans.

In the next few years he did everything he could to set up a business of his own. First it was a snail farm, but the competition was too tough. Then he thought about importing slightly risqué videos. But mainly Muslim Sarajevo was not an ideal market. So he flirted with the idea of setting up a central heating company, but that never got off the ground either. Then there was the Indian shop selling everything from incense to wooden elephants. The economy nose-dived and Indian goods were no longer top of people's shopping list. And still he kept trying. Like Bosnia's Mr Micawber, he believed something 'would eventually turn up'. For me, he embodied the spirit of this country: trying gamely to stand on his own two feet – against the odds.

Sitting on a wooden picnic bench on a hill above Sarajevo, I promised Jonathan that he had nothing to fear and that I would protect his identity. I discreetly pulled the tape recorder out of my bag, talking at the same time, well aware that the sight of a recording machine could make a potential interviewee shy away at the last moment. The cold weather had deterred walkers so there were no prying eyes to witness our meeting. I also promised we would disguise his voice when we broadcast the interview and that his real name would be changed.

Jonathan had finally agreed to speak out. Over the last couple of years our professional relationship had developed into friendship. We trusted each other. I pushed the red Record button. The interview progressed without a hitch, and then we got to the part that I had been waiting for. He'd told me before we started that he would say it, but I did not know if, when the moment came, he actually would go on record.

> They have pinned him down to an area of around sixty to eighty square kilometres. I am not sure whether this is through human intelligence or technical intelligence. Maybe it's a combination of the two. But they are extremely confident that it is him. There is just one problem. It's in Montenegro . . . north-west Montenegro.

This was the most direct Western-sourced information relating to the whereabouts of Karadžić I had ever heard. To give a location and even an area was unprecedented. But there was the very real problem that the location was in another country and it was totally illegal for a military operation to take place there without the express permission of the Montenegrin Government. Even with an agreement, carrying out such a raid could invite enormous political problems. My source was in an extremely privileged position and I trusted what he told me. It seemed that the journeys I had been making to Montenegro – and indeed the very areas I had visited – were right on track. It was time for me to return.

10

Secret Police

'It became apparent that we were being followed. We circled the cemetery and they stayed on our tail. At breakfast, the waitress told us about 20 undercover policemen had been in the hotel since our arrival' – Diary excerpt, 5 August 2005

My German colleague Markus had received similar information about Karadžić's whereabouts from someone very close to the government in Montenegro itself. Cranking my ancient jeep into action again, my fixer Marko and I prepared for another long trek across the mountains. On the way, we passed the restaurant near Foča where Karadžić had allegedly been sighted in April. A Dutch former journalist was reported as having spotted him and his wife having lunch there. A source later told me that the information was 'extremely flaky' and a follow-up investigation found no corroborative evidence.

It took us three hours to reach the remote border point crossing at Šcepan Polje. Our first stop was a remote monastery where Karadžić might well have stopped on his way out of the country. The crumbling road passed down through the Bosnian side, then there was a sharp turn to the right and the road began to rise towards Montenegro. At the bottom, where the road bent right, there was a narrow track to the left, overlooked by trees and steep cliffs, leading to the monastery. It was a remote area. There were few cars and even fewer buildings. As we took the winding track we noticed a battered red car parked next to the mountain road, facing the junction. It seemed an odd place to stop. Slowing, we saw an elderly man with a beard sitting in the driver's seat. He looked over at us and scribbled something in a notebook.

Our route then began to climb and the trees and bushes seemed to close in around us. After a series of hairpin bends we emerged on to a high plain. In front of us, nestling on the edge of the mountain, with a spectacular view over the valley below, was the Monastery of St John the Baptist. Major renovation work seemed to be taking place. There were piles of stones, scaffolding and newly built walls.

Marko went to find someone and returned with a smiling monk who seemed genuinely delighted to see us. He told us about the medieval city that used to exist on the slopes above the monastery and pointed up to the ruins which were still visible. His English was good. In the past he had worked for an advertising agency in London. We asked him what he thought about Karadžić and the claims that he was a war criminal. He said he did not like The Hague Tribunal, did not believe it was bringing justice to the Balkans. But, on the other hand, he did support the recent comments of one of his colleagues who had said that it would be better for the Serb people as a whole if the former Bosnian Serb President handed himself in. He said a Christian's way was 'via the Cross', presumably meaning it was a good thing to sacrifice oneself for others. I asked him bluntly if he believed individuals within the Church could be protecting Karadžić. With a shrug of his shoulders and a lift of his eyebrows, he said, 'Anything is possible.' He gave us a short tour of the monastery but did not wish to engage in any further political discussion.

On our way back we looked out for the red car but it had gone. It was only a few hundred metres to the border point and, after showing our passports, we entered Montenegro. The road, as usual, was virtually empty. The sun was shining, and Marko and I enjoyed the rugged scenery. After an hour or so, we reached the turning for Petnica though our route would take us past it. But as we passed the junction we noticed two men standing next to a red Pajero jeep. They were both wearing Hawaiian shirts and looking directly at us. One of them, who was talking on a mobile phone, hung up as soon as he saw us and both men jumped into their car. As we passed them, the jeep pulled out behind us. For the next half an hour we played cat and mouse with the Pajero. We would pull over by the roadside and let them pass; half a mile further down the road the Pajero would be parked waiting for us. There was no doubt they were tailing us. At one point we saw a grey saloon car parked next to them in a lay-by, its occupants talking to them. As soon as we drove by, the Pajero pulled in behind us on the road.

At we entered the town of Nikšić we reached a roundabout. Slowing down, we let the Pajero come up behind us. Round we went, once, twice, three times. The Pajero stayed on our tail until the driver suddenly realised what was happening and the attention this was attracting from motorists and passers-by. He veered off to the right, shot through some red traffic lights and disappeared out of sight.

Although slightly shaken by this incident we continued as planned to the annex to Ostrog Monastery at Jovan Do. After Nikšić we headed south and the road began to climb. Having crossed a low bridge, we saw a junction ahead. A car was parked in front of us, at the turning to Jovan Do. It was the Pajero.

This time it did not pull out behind us. I kept an eye on the rear-view mirror as we drove higher, but there was no sign of pursuit. And then, suddenly, we found ourselves in front of a huge gate. Set in a natural bowl between rugged hills, the build-ings and church of the Jovan Do complex lay before us. The dormitories and work areas of the monks encircled a field of corn the size of a football pitch. The church's bells suddenly began to chime, as if announcing our arrival. But there was no one around.

We made our way around the field to the church. As we

arrived, a black-robed monk with a black beard emerged. He came over and asked us very formally what we were doing there. As I started to explain, the monk's manner changed. At that moment I realised we recognised each other. He had been at Ostrog on the occasion of the Sveti Vasilije celebration. He told us cordially that he would need to ask the Bishop at Ostrog for permission for us to visit, and made it clear that we would have to leave in the interim.

Half an hour later we were checking into the classic, old-style Communist hotel in the centre of Nikšić. After unpacking, Marko and I went down to reception. As we walked out of the lift, I spotted the two Hawaiian-shirted men checking what looked like the hotel register. We slipped out by a back door and headed into town. But it soon became apparent we had not escaped our pursuers. Two men were following us at a discreet distance. The sunshine had given way to summer rain and at one point I turned round to see a third man, carrying a yellow umbrella, literally jump behind a tree to avoid being seen.

That evening we decided to have dinner in the cavernous restaurant of the hotel. Apart from one man sitting at a table on the far side of the room, but facing in our direction, we were the only guests. Marko began chatting up the middle-aged waitress and the two of them wandered off for a minute or two. When he returned to our table he told me what he had found out: during the previous 48 hours at least 20 plain-clothes policemen had been seen in or around the hotel. Apparently, the other diner was one of them.

Over a dinner of cold meat and potatoes we decided we could not continue like this. Nobody would speak to us under these circumstances. It seemed clear that we were being followed by Montenegro's secret police, but why? Were we perceived as a threat? Were they protecting someone or something they did not want us to find? Or were they following us in the hope that we would lead them somewhere? After a brief discussion, we decided it would be best to grab the bull by the horns.

The next morning it did not take us long to find someone who could give us directions to the office of the secret police. In a town this size it was difficult to keep anything 'secret'. As we arrived at an unmarked building in the centre, we recognised a few of the people who had been following us during the past 24 hours. They were hanging around outside, reading newspapers and smoking. When they saw us, it was impossible for them to conceal their surprise. It was unusual for people to come voluntarily to this place.

We introduced ourselves at the main desk and were told to wait. Twenty minutes later we were ushered into a shabby room on the first floor. At first glance it resembled a down-at-heel Swedish sauna with its cheap wood panelling and fuzzy-screened TV perched on a precarious platform. But there were differences: like the shredding machine behind the desk and strange wires suspended in the air, leading from the desk and disappearing behind a wooden partition behind it. At his large desk, on a chair that seemed to be slightly raised from the ground – presumably to give him some sort of psychological advantage – sat the chief of police. He was middle-aged, lean, with well-groomed hair and a neat grey moustache. He wore a zipped blue T-shirt top and grey trousers. With a tight smile, he indicated we might want to sit down on the ancient armchairs in front of his desk, then he leaned down to fiddle with something in one of his drawers. It was then that I guessed those very visible wires were probably linked to a tape recorder which he was now switching on.

'How can I help you?' he said.

We explained that we had come to Montenegro on the trail of Radovan Karadžić. We were also wondering who was following us and why.

'We do not have any intelligence that he is in this area,' the police chief replied, 'at least, not from our sources. In fact, we have no knowledge of any war crimes fugitives in the region. I would personally go and arrest him if foreign colleagues gave us information about his whereabouts. We've heard rumours about his presence here and we've checked these out. It's a lie that he was at the funeral of his mother,' he added.

'OK, we understand,' I said. 'But why have you sent people to follow us?' We gave him the registration number of the jeep. He copied it down, and promised to find out more.

'They're not working for me,' he said, but could not meet my eye as he spoke. I told him how we had been pursued from the moment we arrived in Montenegro, that we had nothing to hide, and asked if he could he use his influence to stop the harassment. While still refusing to acknowledge his own involvement, he did concede that it was 'unpleasant' to be followed. But he added that it was important for the local authorities to be aware of foreigners who came into the area, and to know what they were doing.

The atmosphere relaxed slightly after that and he offered us a choice of coffee or grape brandy. He carried on drinking what looked like apple juice.

'Journalists have been sucking my blood on this Karadžić issue for a long time,' he confided. Then, 'Don't worry about being followed. There's no reason for it now.'

Before we left, he arranged for us to meet the local police commander covering the Petnica and Šavnik area, who might be able to help us with our quest for Karadžić.

An hour later we were in the police station in Šavnik. The officer in charge looked hesitant as we walked in but managed a tight smile and a firm handshake. As we started asking him questions, he kept referring to the piece of paper he had in front of him. Obviously, he had been briefed in advance.

'It's classic policing here,' he told us. 'It's an isolated area and in winter we deal mainly with things like electricity problems. If Radovan Karadžić or any other criminals came here, I would know.' He also mentioned that there were two monasteries and some churches in the area.

'Would you search a monastery if you had to?' I asked.

He looked shocked.

'Well ... err ... I would have to seek authorisation from above first.'

COUNT 2
(GENOCIDE)

Radovan KARADŽIĆ participated in a joint criminal enterprise to eliminate the Bosnian Muslims in Srebrenica by killing the men and boys of Srebrenica and forcibly removing the women, young children and some elderly men from Srebrenica. Radovan KARADŽIĆ intended to destroy the Bosnian Muslims in Srebrenica as part of the Bosnian Muslim national, ethnical and/or religious group. He shared this intent with other members of this joint criminal enterprise.

Ceasefires came and went as did peace conferences, but there was no breakthrough. In one surreal moment, Karadžić's literary aspirations received a boost when the Russian Writers' Union awarded him the prestigious Mikhail Sholokhov prize for his poetry. A spokesman for the Union said: 'We have studied two volumes of his verse and believe that he is a worthy recipient. The prize is in honour of the humanity and Slavic spirit which permeates his poetry.'

The Russian nationalist writer Eduard Limonov had been a guest of Karadžić in the hills above Sarajevo in 1992 and had been so enthusiastic about the Serb cause he even took to firing a few rounds from a sniper rifle into the city below. In a TV documentary made at the time, Karadžić and Limonov are seen standing on one of the hills above Sarajevo. The Bosnian Serb President looks down at the destroyed buildings below and turns to Limonov. 'There is a poem of mine about Sarajevo,' he tells the Russian writer. 'The first line was: I can hear disaster walking. City is burning out like tamjan [incense] in a church. In this smoke, there is our conscience over there and ... err ... a squad of armed topola, armed trees.' With his mop of hair blowing in the wind and the sounds of firing in the background, Karadžić explains his vision to Limonov. 'Everything I saw armed. Everything I saw in terms of fighting, in terms of war, in army terms. That was 23 years ago that I wrote this poem. And many other poems have something of prediction which frightens me sometimes.'

I hear the misfortune threads
Turned into a beetle as if an old singer
Is crushed by the silence and turned into a voice.

The town burns like a piece of incense
In the smoke rumbles our consciousness.
Empty suits slide down the town.
Red is the stone that dies, built into a house. The Plague!

Calm. The army of armed poplar tree
Marches up the hill, within itself.
The aggressor air storms our souls
and once you are human and then you are an air
    creature.

I know that all of these are the preparations of the scream:
What does the black metal in the garage have for us?
Look how fear turned into a spider
Looking for the answer at his computer.

Another of his more well-known poems, 'Mad Spear', begins:

Measure your steps, your hand's twists
That spear you throw is mad
The landscapes awaiting it are full of no names and no
    reason.

Something like a chill is nesting within you
That spear, that stretched arm, glows in your head
You feel that mortal metal, its presence
You don't think of it and it is still a metal.

*By 1994 Karadžić himself probably felt the chill as his personal position
came under increasing pressure. Relations with his one-time patron,
Slobodan Milošević, had been shaky ever since the Bosnian Serb Parliament had rejected the Vance-Owen plan. By August 1994 Milošević was
becoming openly hostile to the Bosnian Serb leader, as witnessed by the*

increasingly anti-Karadžić commentaries in the Belgrade media, largely under the regime's control.

The daily newspaper Politika *wrote: 'Once peace comes, the people cannot be led by the men who bombarded civilians in Sarajevo and those who, to the world's revulsion, promoted their poetry over Sarajevo while the city was burning.'*

Feeling increasingly isolated, the Bosnian Serb leader told the Bosnian Serbs: 'Now we are totally, totally alone, only God is with us.' By October 1994 The Times *was reporting that an attempted coup in Republika Srpska had been crushed by those loyal to Karadžić. His gradual isolation continued, then in April 1995 the pressure increased dramatically when the then Chief Prosecutor at The Hague, Judge Richard Goldstone, said he was investigating Karadžić for alleged war crimes. A few months later he was formally indicted.*

This followed the single most infamous event of the Bosnian War: the massacre of Srebrenica. Later, in an interview for The Times *in February 1996, Karadžić would say: 'There was no order to kill them. Nobody under my command would dare kill those who were arrested or captured as prisoners-of-war.'*

But Srebrenica was the beginning of the end for the Bosnian Serb war machine. When news of the massacre began to emerge it crystallised in one bloody event the whole terror and horror that was the Bosnian War. Karadžić's daughter Sonja, who was her father's Press Secretary at the time, told me: 'It was two or three days after the fall of the town that journalists began ringing and asking if we knew what was going on. They had been talking to peasants in villages near Srebrenica. The peasants said that they had heard some shooting and screams during the night . . . I called my father and told him that we had heard from two or three sides, not connected to journalists, that something was going on. He said that he would immediately try to find General Mladić.'

'When did he realise the scale of what had happened at Srebrenica?' I asked her.

'I don't know exactly, but I know that that was after journalists called me.'

'Did your father know before or during that thousands of Muslim men were being killed?'

'No, absolutely not.'

It was unclear when or what Karadžić had known of these events. But what was in no doubt was that he was the Supreme Commander of Bosnian Serb forces and, as such, he could not deny his responsibility.

Our tiny helicopter swooped low over the forest. The side door was wide open so that my cameraman could film properly. Our feet were hanging out of the cabin. At one point, my cameraman realised that his seatbelt was unfastened and a soldier had to climb across him to fix it. As the helicopter banked to one side to get a better angle of the buildings below, my stomach heaved.

Lord Ashdown had promised there would be a co-ordinated attack on the support network allegedly protecting war crimes fugitives and believed to be supported by organised crime. One of their key businesses was illegal logging. Much of Bosnia was covered in forest and many areas had been totally devastated by the actions of illegal logging companies. The EUFOR peacekeepers had decided to try to tackle the issue by setting up roadblocks, examining the lorries transporting wood and interrogating the drivers. The aim was to squeeze the war crimes fugitives where it hurt most: their funding.

The EUFOR helicopter had been made available to us so we could write a story about illegal loggers operating in the region around Sarajevo. We made several stops along the way. At one point we landed on a football pitch on the outskirts of a town and made a short trip to one of the unlicensed saw mills. Bemused workers stood and watched as the owners were questioned while we filmed from a discreet distance. This campaign was an explicit sign of intent and it had some success. But was it having any real impact on the war crimes issue?

The Metropolitan threaded black prayer beads through his hands as he stared into my eyes with his unnerving gaze. His black robe, long grey beard and gold chain with its medallion depicting Mary and Jesus proclaimed his authority as a senior cleric of the Serbian Orthodox Church. Black-robed deputies surrounded him, sitting under the trees of the monastery garden where nuns were serving refreshments. The hot summer sun was high in the sky. Amfilohije Radović, head of the Serbian Church in Montenegro, was perfectly at ease, laughing often and apparently open to all conversational gambits and banter. This was the first official interview he had given to a foreign journalist for ten years.

The setting could hardly have been more idyllic: the eighteenth-century Brceli Monastery, tucked away in the verdant hills, not far from the coast in Montenegro. A monk filmed us on a home video camera. 'For the Metropolitan's personal archive,' I was told.

'So, what type of man was . . . and is . . . Radovan Karadžić?' I asked him.

'Radovan comes from an old, respected Montenegrin family from Durmitor. He is a psychiatrist and poet,' said Amfilohije. 'His mother Jovanka, who was buried recently, told me once: "I said to Radovan, 'You're a doctor and a poet and you shouldn't go into politics.'" But he became a politician and got very involved and mixed up in a civil war, like a continuation of the Second World War in many ways . . . the disintegration of the state, irrational enmities. In a sense this time has eaten up this man. I know him personally. He seems like a normal man and essentially he likes his profession as a doctor.'

I took a sip from my glass of grape brandy. 'But what type of man is he? What are his strengths and his weaknesses?'

The Metropolitan took his time over answering. 'What person doesn't have weaknesses?' he asked eventually. 'But he is a normal person, and in normal times you would expect him to act normally. But these were not normal times and normal events. And the most normal people can completely lose . . . their senses.'

'He lost his senses?'

'It's possible . . . it's possible. It's not an easy situation to deal with. Honestly speaking, it's not easy for me to deal with the situation . . . although it's easier now.'

'Is he a war criminal?'

'Until the court decides, no one can be considered a criminal. But even after the worldly courts condemn someone, it
is not absolutely certain. That's why the last judgement belongs
to God. I'll give you one example . . . maybe it's not an adequate
comparison. Take Christ. The normal state court of a big and
powerful Empire condemned him as a criminal and he was
crucified. But today all normal people cannot live without the
crucified one. That doesn't mean this applies to Karadžić, I
just wanted to point out that justice from wordly courts is
relative.'

'His wife asks him to go to The Hague. Do you support
this?'

'I personally think the decision should be left to him. His
wife has asked him to give up because she and her family feel
threatened. And there is all this pressure from the media.
Terrible pressure. It's very hard to put up with all of that. I
wouldn't know what I would do if I were in his place. I can't
say what he should do, but I can say what I would do. I would
go to The Hague.'

'Why?'

'I am a monk. I couldn't care if I was in prison or in a
monastery. I belong to Christ.'

'But if you were him, you wouldn't be a monk.'

'That's true,' he laughed.

'If he'd asked you for help, would you have given it to him?'

'The last time I saw him was 1995. He hasn't contacted me
or asked me for anything. If he had contacted me, I can't say
how I would have reacted. But in any case, I would try to help
him as I would help you or any other man – as a Christian
and as a monk. Anything I could do. What I would consider
it my Christian duty to do.'

I asked again if he thought Karadžić should hand himself
in and go to The Hague.

'This is his personal decision. He is a sensible man. Not a
stupid man at all. He's an intellectual. As I wouldn't want
someone to impose their will on me, I wouldn't like to do the
same to him. But I expect him to make that decision, as he

took responsibility for leading the Serbs from Bosnia – even though he is a Serb from Montenegro – I expect him to do the right thing, taking such responsibility upon himself. Then it has full value.

'I had the opportunity of speaking to some people who are now in The Hague before they left. When they asked me what I thought, I said, "This is your decision. You have to decide. I can only say what I would do in your place. I would go." And it's possible that some of them left because I told them that . . . This is a question of personal responsibility in front of God, the people and history.'

I asked him then about Jovan Do and whether Karadžić was sheltering in Church property. He denied it.

'Do you categorically call for him to go to The Hague, for the sake of the Serbs?'

'I don't know where he is, but if he made this decision himself that would be the right decision.'

'And if you were him, you would go?'

'Yes. In this present situation, I would.'

'Do you know someone who knows where he is?'

'I don't know one person. No, actually, I do know one person who certainly knows – God. I personally really don't. I only know one person who does – that is God.'

'Could you just pretend to abandon your clerical robes for a moment?' I said, with a smile on my face. There was a shuffling in their chairs from the monks looking on. 'And, for a moment, imagine yourself as a journalist.' Smiles all round, and even laughter from my host and his cameraman.

'Imagine you are a journalist and you can ask Radovan Karadžić one question. What would it be?'

The prelate paused for a second then said, 'I would ask him . . . I would ask him . . . did he prefer to live in a hole, like a hunted animal, or would he prefer to go to The Hague and hand himself in?'

But before we left the monastery, the contact who had set up the interview went over to Metropolitan Amfilohije and I could see them having a heated discussion. Immediately afterwards my interviewee came over and said to me: 'If Karadžić is eventually found on Church property, it doesn't mean that we are protecting him. In this world of miracles, anything is possible.' He would not elaborate further. I asked him if we could visit Jovan Do and he said he could be happy to accompany us the following day. We said we would think about it.

On the way back to the hotel, I reflected on the idea of a trip around Jovan Do in the company of the Metropolitan. Even if Karadžić were there now, he would be long gone by the time I appeared. What story would I write then? How we had missed our big opportunity? I decided to decline the offer of the tour.

But before we left Montenegro, I interviewed a senior member of the Montenegrin Government. In an off-the-record comment at the end of our meeting, he confirmed to me that Western intelligence agencies from the United States, Britain and France were on the ground in Montenegro, actively trying to pinpoint the location of Karadžić. But he would say no more – it was unclear whether this was because he'd told us everything he knew or whether he did not wish to compromise an ongoing operation.

In Sarajevo's upmarket suburb of Ilidža, in the shadow of Mount Igman, the police had arrested what were believed to be two Muslim suicide bombers. It was October 2005. Diplomatic sources told me that this was the first time such an incident had occurred and that they were extremely concerned. Apparently, the suicide belts had been 'ready to go', a martyr-style video message had also been recorded, and other weapons and explosives were found. The suicide bombers were two young Bosnian Muslims with citizenship from other European countries.

The vast majority of Bosnia's Muslims have no sympathy for fanatical Islam and abhor violence. However, there had been concern for some time that Bosnia was a potential staging post for extremists – if not from the country itself, then from the Middle East. During the war a number of Muslim fighters had come to Bosnia to join the mainly Muslim Government forces. Some of these were believed to have had links to extremist groups in Afghanistan and elsewhere. After the war, money had been invested by some Middle Eastern countries in Bosnia and there were worries that, with the country's extremely porous borders and prevalence of corruption, extremists might be able to operate there. But there had been no real evidence of it – until now.

During the next few days further arrests took place in Denmark and London. It was claimed those later arrests were linked to the first two people detained. It was not known who those in Bosnia were targeting – or, if it was known, the information was not made public. One diplomat told me that Bosnia was regarded as the R&R (rest and recovery) country for Al-Qaeda.

On 7 July of that same year a terrorist attack in London by suicide bombers, targeting the transport system, left 52 victims dead. As one intelligence contact said: what was more important for a Western government – devoting resources to tracking down the former Bosnian Serb leader who, despite the moral imperative, posed no direct threat to anyone, or devoting those same resources to the fight against potential terrorist groups who did pose a real and direct threat to Western countries?

11

Divided Land

'The day of the funeral dawned drizzly and grey. Marko and I set up position next to the steps of the Federal Parliament and behind the stage. By 11.30 there were thousands in the square, mostly in their forties, fifties and sixties, carrying portraits of their hero. Some had tears in their eyes. The coffin carrying Slobodan Milošević's body was covered in a Serbian flag as it was brought up on stage' – Diary excerpt, 18 March 2006

As many as 50,000 people filled the streets and the park outside the green-domed Federal Parliament waiting to bid a last farewell to a leader who had marched their country through the wars, economic sanctions and international isolation of the 1990s. A few days previously Slobodan Milošević had been found dead in his cell in The Hague. The official line was that he had died of a heart attack, but the rumour mill was in full swing in Belgrade. Allegations of poisoning and murder were common currency, especially among the ranks of his supporters filling the square. One banner read: 'NATO kills by bombing. Its tribunal kills by denying medical care.'

I had heard of Milošević's death while sitting in a shopping-centre car park in Sarajevo. An American journalist friend had sent a two-word text: 'Slobo dead'. From then on my phone did not stop ringing as editors from London wanted reports and updates, on the hour, every hour. A week later I was in the main square in Belgrade. The emotional and angry crowd wanted to make clear not only how much they had admired their former leader, but also how much they despised the West for the way it had treated him.

The atmosphere was tense. Journalistic colleagues, broadcasting from a tent opposite the stage, had already been forced to withdraw after they had attracted the anger of the crowd. Bottles had been thrown at them and it looked for a while as if things could turn even nastier. The BBC was not popular with most of Milošević's supporters who blamed it for everything from the Serb defeat during the Bosnian War to the NATO bombing campaign over Kosovo and now the 'murder' of Milošević in The Hague. The BBC, in their view, was just part of a wider international conspiracy to demonise the Serbs and, in particular, their late, great President. I had been aware that we might face some hostility so had positioned myself in a less conspicuous place, behind the stage where Milošević's coffin was lying, and was able to continue reporting as the funeral orations turned into political speeches.

A large video screen relayed images to the huge crowd. Some people climbed trees to get a better view. 'As long as Serbia and Serbs are alive, Slobodan Milošević will not die,' declared one speaker from the stage. The crowd chanted: 'We'll never let Kosovo go. We'll never let Kosovo go.' Others simply chanted, 'Slobo! Slobo!'

I asked one man why he was there. 'I came here to pay my respects to a great leader,' came the reply. 'He stood up for what he believed in. He was killed by The Hague, by Great Britain and the United States. He was a great man. Today, I feel sad, very sad.'

'I came to say goodbye to the greatest son of Serbia,' said a woman with tears in her eyes, holding up a portrait of her hero.

When the ceremony drew to a close, the former President's coffin was placed in a hearse and the funeral convoy set off on the last leg of its journey to Milošević's home town of Požarevac, a 45-minute drive south from the capital. He was finally laid to rest in the garden of the family home, under the tree where he had once courted the woman who became his wife, Mirjana Marković. A simple granite slab carved with his name and the dates 1941–2006 marked the spot. Serbia's government had refused to allow the ex-leader a state funeral, and Mirjana, on the run in Russia after being charged by Prosecutors in Serbia, did not attend.

Although Milošević was gone, he'd left a very potent legacy. A substantial number of Serbs still believed in the philosophy and policies of their former leader. These people were still locked in the mindset of the past, believing that there was some dastardly, Western-inspired reason for every misfortune that had been visited upon the former Yugoslavia. It was going to be very difficult to persuade such people that reform was a good thing and that there could be a better future, especially those who retained powerful positions in present-day Serbian society. They had their own personal interests to protect.

Serbia was a deeply divided country. The coalition of pro-Democratic parties that had finally ousted Milošević in October 2000 had long since split amidst anger and recrimination. The political landscape was dividing into two separate political camps. There were the nationalists, from hard-line to moderate, who tended to look to the past and stress national injustices. They viewed Russia as a closer ally than the West, and wished to defend war crimes fugitives. The reformists, on the other hand, saw membership of the European Union as a key strategic objective and, crucially, wanted to resolve the war crimes issue so that Serbia could draw a line under its past. This polarisation was not as clearly defined as it was to become later, when the issue of Kosovo's independence would dominate the political arena. But at the time of Milošević's funeral it was already clearly visible.

A few weeks after that I heard from London that I would from now on be based permanently in Belgrade, rather than Sarajevo. After three and a half years, it was clear that the main political and economic stories would centre around the Serbian capital.

I moved into a flat in the old district, not far from Kalemegdan Park. It was a little shabby with a view from the back of a half-built tower block that seemed to have been taken over by the entire population of Belgrade's stray cats. The landlady told me that the flat opposite mine had once been used by Milošević during the 1999 NATO bombing. Apparently, he had changed accommodation every night to avoid being targeted. I tried to imagine the former President travelling up in my lift, looking at himself in the mirror and reading the graffiti on the walls.

The area was mainly residential. With its tree-lined streets, trendy cafes and bars, it attracted the more affluent of Belgrade's citizens. A road not far from mine was known as 'silicon valley', since it was frequented by those in search of various forms of enhancement through plastic surgery. Mobsters and their molls were regular visitors to the neighbourhood.

Lord Ashdown had left Bosnia a few months previously, at the end of January. In one of the last interviews he gave, he said, 'Insofar as it's the international community's job to arrest the former Bosnian Serb leaders Radovan Karadžić and Ratko Mladić, then it's been a failure. There's no other word for it. It's a point that I regret greatly.'

In those spring months, as temperatures began to rise and fascination with my new city took hold, Belgrade seemed a pleasant and lively place to be, especially as a journalist. In just a few months I interviewed leading politicians on the issue of Kosovo's independence. I met His Royal Highness Crown Prince Alexander II of Serbia and Yugoslavia, the British-born head of the royal family. I went once again to Montenegro to witness the final break-up of the former Yugoslavia when the people of Montenegro voted to end their union with Serbia. The six republics of the former Yugoslavia had become six new states.

In the summer evenings I wandered around the park with its spectacular views over the Rivers Danube and Sava which met below the ramparts of the old Turkish fort. I would sit on a park bench and watch the street hawkers selling T-shirts with pictures of Karadžić and Mladić.

I remember one evening about 11 p.m. I was wandering down Knez Mihaijlova, the main pedestrian street in the centre of Belgrade. A few strollers were making a trip to the late-night bookshop near the park. In an alcove, not far away, a street-vendor lit a cigarette. He was tall with cropped hair and was wearing a green, military-style jacket. His was the only stall still open at this time. I ambled closer and looked at what he was selling. There were glossy colour pictures of Radovan Karadžić and Ratklo Mladić, and other nationalist parapher-nalia. He asked me if I wanted to buy anything and I politely declined, my Serbian giving away the fact that I was not local. He just stared at me. In the heart of Belgrade no one was stopping him from plying his business and presumably there must have been enough customers to make it worthwhile. I drifted away.

I read the graffiti on the walls of the university, glorifying Vojislav Šešelj, leader of the Serbian Radicals, whose farewell rally I had witnessed in Republic Square three years previously and who was now in The Hague awaiting trial.

I remember strolling down a backstreet near the Danube and seeing Luka Karadžić, Radovan's brother, going some-where in a hurry. I half-heartedly followed him for a while, wondering if he might be on his way to a secret meeting with his brother, but lost him in the narrow streets. Radovan Karadžić had all but disappeared from the newspaper headlines now. Even Del Ponte had gone quiet. I started to wonder . . .

Richard Gere, Hollywood star, international sex symbol and campaigner for a free Tibet, wiped his nose, glanced over his shoulder and turned back to me. I had just asked him what he thought of Sarajevo and was waiting patiently for his reply.

We were in Baščaršija, the old Turkish quarter of Sarajevo, during a short break while the extras were being briefed and the cameras repositioned. Hollywood had finally come to town to make a film about the hunt for Radovan Karadžić. Gere was playing a journalist on his trail. The irony was not lost on me. Filming had already taken place in Croatia. Now they were spending a couple of weeks in Bosnia to complete the picture. I had been given five minutes with the superstar before he had to shoot his next scene.

'So, what do you think of Sarajevo then?' I tried again.

'Well . . . Sarajevo is a great city and the women are very beautiful,' he ventured diplomatically.

'And do you think . . .' I began. But before I could continue, one of the producers ran up to Gere and pulled him aside. After a hushed conversation, and without any explanation, they walked off together. That was it. My one and only interview with a Hollywood film star.

The film's plot was loosely based on the true story of how a number of journalists had spent some time looking for Karadžić a few years previously, with the aim of receiving the $5 million reward offered by the United States Government. At the start of filming, Gere had given a news conference in which he had expressed a desire to meet the former Bosnian Serb leader:

> I think we have a lot to learn from them [people like Karadžić], why they are the way they are. And why we are so vulnerable to them that we can get sucked into their world view and become violent. I think we're all capable of that, doing horrible things. So I think there is much to learn from these guys.

The arrival of a Hollywood film crew and movie star was a welcome boost to the local economy and added a little buzz to daily city life. But, crucially, it also put the whole issue of Karadžić in the public spotlight once again, at a time when it had started to drift off the international agenda.

Very few journalists were still interested in the story, governments had moved on to different issues, and specialist military resources had been allocated to other crises around the world. There was an excellent blog called findingkaradzic.com and the occasional significant article by old Yugoslav war journalists like Ed Vulliamy and Anthony Loyd. Numerous but increasingly irrelevant raids were made by peacekeepers in Bosnia on the alleged support networks sustaining war crimes fugitives. Little of any value was ever found on them. The hunt for Karadžić was now virtually non-existent. The trail had gone cold.

Karadžić had been excluded from the negotiations which led to the Dayton Peace Agreement and the end of the war, because he had been indicted by the UN War Crimes Tribunal and also because it was felt that it was better to deal with Slobodan Milošević rather than the Bosnian Serb leadership. By the early-winter of 1995 it was clear that the war was coming to an end, and it was just a matter of time before all parties realised that peace was in the best interests of everyone. Questions were already being asked about what a post-war Bosnia would be like and, in particular, what would happen to the Bosnian Serb leaders, especially Karadžić and Mladić. Would they be arrested and sent to The Hague? In a BBC interview in November 1995 Karadžić warned against any attempt to arrest him:

> *If they try to arrest me . . . not only me but any single citizen of my country . . . there is going to be bloodshed. There are going to be many, many dead Western soldiers and that will be a terrible nightmare for the Western armies here. I have my army and my guards and they would save me. But let me ask you why they should arrest me? The Dayton Agreement has legalised and legitimised our fight for freedom and for our own state or let's say entity.*

He was asked if he was guilty of war crimes.

> *No, sir, I am President and I make my decisions and give my orders that are all known and public and we have never issued any wrong order. At the beginning of the war I issued the strongest order to my commanders to stick to the Geneva Convention and all of them have it in their own pockets.*

He tried to keep a low profile but everyone knew that he was spending most of his time at home in Pale or in his office a short distance away, protected by his well-armed bodyguards. NATO troops were stationed nearby but no attempt was made to take him into custody. It seemed that the President's bravado warning was enough to deter any such operation.

By July 1996 Karadžić was causing so many headaches to the US administration that the Dayton negotiator, Richard Holbrooke, was sent back to the Balkans. In a later interview with Neil McDonald from the Financial Times, *Holbrooke described what happened:*

I went back to Belgrade, this time as a private citizen, as a special envoy for Clinton with a mission to get Karadžić out of public life. Now it was my deep preference that we arrest him but rather than arrest him I was told . . . you know, that time he was still operating in the open from his office in Pale. The NATO commander did not wish to arrest him, and instead of confronting the NATO commander and ordering him to arrest him, the Administration sent me on a shuttle between Belgrade and Sarajevo and, shuttling back and forth, we got Karadžić to sign a piece of paper giving up his two titles: President of Republika Srpska and President of the SDS Party, and an agreement that he would disappear from public life. He was of course not in Belgrade for that negotiation but in the middle of the night Stanišić [Jovica Stanišić was Milošević's Head of the State Security Service. He was subsequently put on trial at The Hague accused of murder, persecutions, deportation and inhuman acts] flew down to Pale by helicopter and got him to sign it while we were waiting and came back to Belgrade with the signature and so he disappeared from public life . . .

He got nothing, of course not. He simply withdrew. He just quit his two jobs and agreed to have no more public role. There was no discussion of an amnesty or anything like that, not at all. So he signed it and maybe, you know, who knows what Milošević and Stanišić told him that night? But there was no deal. And he put out the story that he had a deal and then they came up with this extraordinary forged piece of paper . . . which is the crudest forgery which shows a signature not remotely resembling mine and forged Karadžić's signature and someone else's saying that there was

*this deal and that the US would provide him with a security detail
and money and $600,000 a year.*

*It's hilarious and why anyone would take the word of an indicted
war criminal – and a man who has famously said that the Muslims
attacked their own market-place in order to lure NATO into
the war – over that of the United States, a country which shit
blood and treasure to resolve these problems down here, is beyond
comprehension. But because NATO failed in its responsibility to
arrest and locate these two guys, and because Karadžić is an adept
practitioner of disinformation, the story took root.*

Karadžić did eventually withdraw and his place as RS President was
taken by his former Deputy, Biljana Plavšić. 'My father called us into
his office, late in the evening, I think it was 18 July 1996, and told us
that he'd finally made a deal and that now he didn't have to be worried
about The Hague,' recalls Sonja Karadžić. Her mother insists there was
a deal: 'Radovan told me that he reached a deal, some kind of gentlemen's
agreement, as he liked to say.'

From then on Karadžić is thought to have stayed mainly in Pale and
was occasionally spotted in town. But no attempt at all was made to
detain him. He did have some contact with foreigners, for instance
William Stuebner who had worked in a senior capacity for a number of
organisations, including the ICTY and the OSCE (Organisation for
Security and Co-operation in Europe).

'I met him for the last time in May 1997. I was a private citizen
having resigned from the OSCE and not yet having returned to the
ICTY,' said Stuebner. 'I talked with him about possible surrender and
he seriously considered it, but feared that Milošević agents in his guard
force would kill him and blame NATO.' Stuebner believes he went into
hiding in the summer of 1997. 'I think he felt that if he were too public,
NATO would feel obliged to arrest him. They may have told him this.'

The international community was initially reluctant to start arresting
those wanted by The Hague. But then there was a change in policy.

'During the winter and spring of 1997, there was a genuine discussion
in key countries on the need to start arresting [fugitives],' the former chief
international civilian representative to Bosnia, Swedish diplomat Carl
Bildt, told me. 'One issue was whether to start from the top – Karadžić

– or with the smaller people. I argued we should start with the top because otherwise Karadžić and others would immediately disappear after having seen the new policy, and it would be extremely difficult after that for us. But the political decision was to start at the bottom end.'

In April 1998 it emerged that Karadžić was no longer in his house. His guards had also vanished. When journalists asked where he was, they were simply told that he had left. But no one would give a precise date when or say where he had gone. From this time onwards, until he was eventually captured, only the odd unsubstantiated sighting would be reported. In the winter of 1997–8, to all intents and purposes, Radovan Karadžić disappeared from the face of the earth.

'There was a secret deal. I saw the document with my own eyes,' said the man sitting opposite me in a backstreet restaurant in Belgrade. He twisted the large gold ring on his left index finger and glanced out of the window. 'It was in August 1995, late-afternoon. The meeting took place in the Serbian Presidency building. It was just as preparations were taking place for the Dayton peace talks in the United States.'

Speculation about the alleged immunity deal between Radovan Karadžić and Richard Holbrooke refused to die. Karadžić's supporters continued to insist that an agreement had been made. Holbrooke vehemently denied it. In the absence of any precise evidence one way or the other and the continuing freedom of the former Bosnian Serb President, the conspiracy theorists kept resurrecting the allegations. I wanted to examine these claims more closely for myself. In October 2007, I had the opportunity.

The man I was meeting was Vladimir Nadezdin, a former senior official in the Milošević regime during the mid-1990s. He had been one of the Serbian negotiating team at Dayton. He arrived early at the restaurant, evidently keen to tell me his story. I asked him to give me a description of what exactly he saw.

'The piece of paper was in A4 format with the official logo of the Bosnian Serb Republic and the President of the Republic,' he replied without hesitation. I handed him a pen and he started drawing it in my notebook.

'The first point was about Mr Karadžić giving up his political functions, the second one was about his withdrawal from party functions.

'The third one was about withdrawal from public life, and the last one, which was the most important one, was that Radovan Karadžić would not be under the jurisdiction of The Hague.'

'Who was at the meeting?' I asked.

'There was President Milošević and our Foreign Minister, Milan Milutinović. For the Americans there was Holbrooke and Wesley Clarke. Holbrooke produced the paper from an inside pocket of his jacket. I was shown the document by Milutinović for whom I was working at the time.'

'Where is the document now?'

'It was supposed to be archived by the Ministry of Foreign Affairs. But that has been officially denied. I don't know where it is now.'

If the document really did exist, no one seemed to know where it was. But this fact had not deterred The Hague from quietly encouraging War Crimes Prosecutors in Belgrade to investigate the matter.

In January 2007, Serbia had gone to the polls in a General Election. The hard-line nationalist Serbian Radical Party won the largest number of seats in Parliament but, after the usual months of negotiations between the pro-democratic parties, the latter formed a government. The nationalist Prime Minister, Vojislav Koštunica, kept his position despite the differences he had with President Boris Tadić, while Tadić's Democratic Party took over key positions in the government, including Defence and Foreign Affairs. But there were continuous pressures within the coalition, especially as the issue of Kosovo rose to the top of the political agenda.

In April, I interviewed Tadić in the Presidency building, in the busy centre of Belgrade. The last time I had interviewed him it had been in the wake of the Djindjic assassination. His career had flourished since those days and his new grey hair reflected the mounting pressures and new responsibilities. This time he did have advisers with him and they had obviously briefed him on interview techniques in order to improve his public image. Just before we started, the President suddenly got up from his comfortable armchair.

'Sorry, I have forgotten something,' he explained.

A minute later he came back carrying another cushion. He placed it on top of the cushion already in his chair and sat down. 'It just looks better on camera,' he confided to me with a smile and a signal that he was ready to start.

I questioned him about general political developments but also took him to task on the issue of war crimes. Why, I asked him, had the remaining fugitives still not been arrested?

'First of all,' he replied, 'I have to say that we're facing real difficulties in finding all those indicted here in Serbia and the region. Second, in the past seven years we've co-operated with The Hague Tribunal in a very efficient way. And we have good-will to finalise this co-operation, in the next few days, weeks, months, but, from time to time, we're faced with real technical difficulties.'

'What technical difficulties?'

'The Ministry of the Interior . . . this is not very easy, to find all the indicted. Even though the international perception is that this is a very easy process, this is not the case.'

He would not say any more. To me this was another clear example of the deep divisions that still existed between the political and security systems. Just as the country was divided about its future, so the power structures failed to speak with one voice.

In the same month I returned to the United Kingdom and arranged to see Paddy Ashdown in the House of Lords. After a warm handshake and a brisk march through the metal detectors, he led me to the Lords' cafeteria.

'Tea and scones?' he asked, ordering them before I had a chance to reply. Ushering me over to a table for two, he told me he believed we were now further away from catching Karadžić than at any time in the previous decade.

'He's probably still flitting between Bosnia and Montenegro. But I don't know much more than that. In the past there were resources available . . . The world has changed. They are no longer available.'

'And what's your assessment? Who is protecting him?' I asked.

'You can't rule out anyone. Maybe some nations helped him in the past. Maybe the Church. We just do not know for sure.'

He was genuinely concerned that Karadžić would never be found. After we'd finished our tea and scones, I was shown out as quickly as I had been shown in.

Why did I continue to pursue Radovan Karadžić? What was the point? Wasn't he consigned to history now? Was it not time for me to move on? But every now and then I would meet someone who would remind me why the story was so important. It could be looking into the eyes of the smiling and cheerful Sabina who had been raped in front of her children; or talking to the angry widow from Srebrenica who wanted not only to find the bodies of her loved ones, but believed there should be 'justice' for what had happened to her and her family; or the Serb teacher who was forced to dig trenches on the frontline and brutalised by his guards. The tragedy and the sorrow were as endless as the memories.

Damir was sitting in an armchair opposite me. He had a full head of reddish-orange hair and a big moustache to match. He worked at the local petrol station in a village half an hour's drive from Sarajevo. Now he was telling me about why he was the luckiest person to be alive. At the beginning of the war, he was working at a filling station in the town of Višegrad.

'We hid in the woods and watched as our village was burned to the ground by Serb paramilitaries. We could hear the gunfire as people were shot.' Along with dozens of others who had fled their homes, he was eventually persuaded to leave the forest and promised transport out of Bosnia.

There were fifty of us on a bus. We had originally been told we would be going to Macedonia but then the plan changed and we were told we were to be exchanged for Serb prisoners. But then the beatings started and I gradually began to fear that we were not going to be exchanged at all. After hours on the bus we were driven up a small hill and then let off the bus. We were marched off in a column, two by two. I was at the back. Our hands were tied behind our backs with wire. There was still a glimmer of hope that we were being exchanged – we were not far from the front line.

But then the first two were called forward. They were standing close to a bush, about twenty metres away from me. They were shot at point-blank range. Their bodies tumbled forwards into what I later discovered was a cave, hidden by the bush. The rest of us froze. There was no shouting, no panic, no crying, just total paralysis. They had executed ten of us, most of them friends and relatives of mine. The Serb commander ordered the two guards at the back of the line to go forward and take part in the killings. I said to myself, 'This is it, this is it.' I turned and began to run, my hands still tied. I made six or seven metres before I felt the warmth of the bullets passing me. After thirty metres, I fell into some leaves and glanced back. I couldn't see anyone following. I got up and kept on running.

It was another four hours before Damir found sanctuary in a Muslim village. He had escaped unscathed. Six years later he brought investigators from the ICTY to the scene of the killings. Inside the cave, they found 49 bodies. Damir, the fiftieth person to be detained, was the only survivor, the only witness.

A powerful heatwave hit the Balkans during the summer of 2007. In Belgrade temperatures soared to 45°C. Water tankers were placed on the streets to provide drinking supplies. Rivers dried up. Forest fires broke out everywhere. The government confirmed that a large part of the harvest was destroyed.

I spent my time making a music documentary about the rise and fall of so-called 'Turbo Folk' – a style of music combining traditional music with thrashy, electronic beats. But what really distinguished Turbo Folk was the overt sexuality and brash lifestyle that its performers and their lyrics glorified. Short-skirted singers, flashy cars and bling abounded. This music and imagery had provided much-needed escapism during the troubled 1990s. Its greatest exponent was Svetlana Ražnatović, known as 'Ceca', who was married to the infamous Serbian paramilitary, Arkan. The rise and fall of Turbo Folk went hand in hand with the rise and fall of Milošević.

During the final months of 2007, the coalition government began to wobble. Koštunica was making Kosovo the government's number one issue; he was keen to preserve it within Serbia's boundaries, whatever the cost. Tadić's Democrats also believed Kosovo should remain within Serbia, but their number one priority was the European Union. Before the internal conflict came to a head, Serbia held a Presidential election in January 2008. It was portrayed as a referendum on the country's future: whether it was to move closer to Russia under the leadership of the hard-line nationalist Tomislav Nikolić, or whether the country was to ally itself with the European Union. After a second round of voting, Tadić narrowly defeated his challenger. But tensions remained high. Two weeks later, the pressure that had been building up finally exploded when the majority ethnic Albanian population in Kosovo declared independence from Serbia. Kosovo was the historical and religious heartland of Serbia. Although most Serbs had never even visited their southern province, it had a tremendous emotional pull. It was unthinkable to most Serbs that Kosovo could now be an independent state. Major EU countries and the United States immediately recognised the new state. Kosovo, like the war crimes issue, became a rallying point for nationalists. For many Serbs, Kosovo was another example of the perfidious West trying to humiliate mother Serbia.

We were hiding in the apartment. We had switched off the lights, turned down the volume on the TV and locked the doors. Outside, the mob roamed the streets looking for victims. We could hear the smashing of shop windows and the chants of the crowd. I peeped out of the window and watched as the rioters crossed the park below, waving flags, swigging alcohol and throwing trash cans into the street. I could see the smoke rising from the direction of the United States Embassy.

It was 21 February 2008, just four days after the declaration of Kosovo's independence. Tens of thousands of people had poured into the square outside the old Federal Parliament building in Belgrade to protest against Kosovo's declaration of independence. The nationalist Prime Minister, Vojislav Koštunica, who had campaigned relentlessly but futilely against independence, gave an impassioned speech condemning the move by the ethnic Albanians. Tadić and the reformers were nowhere to be seen, preferring to express their opposition to Kosovo's independence elsewhere.

Several colleagues and I had positioned ourselves in an apartment overlooking the rally. We were warned not to wander in the crowd speaking English. One of the targets of the protestors were the countries that had recognised Kosovo.

As the rally came to an end and darkness began to fall, around a thousand protestors marched off in the direction of the district where most Western embassies were situated. Once there, they proceeded to attack the embassies throwing rocks, spraying graffiti, smashing windows. The United States Embassy was the focal point. Inexplicably, no Serbian anti-riot police had been deployed to protect it. Encouraged by the lack of police, the rioters lay siege to the Embassy and soon built up enough courage to climb into the compound and set fire to part of the building. In the basement, US security officials made urgent phone calls asking for assistance.

The apartment I was in was just a few blocks from the US Embassy. I watched live pictures on television as the flames licked the walls of the Embassy. Suddenly, the pictures showed Serbian riot-police racing up the street in armoured cars. The demonstrators, many covering their faces with scarves, moved away. I realised they were being forced back in the direction of the square below our apartment. I went to the window and saw Serbian journalists below quickly packing their gear and getting into their vehicles.

Our balcony was covered in lights and cameras. One of my colleagues was on live television. Suddenly I heard shouts from the other side of the square and saw hooded youths heading in our direction. There was still no sign of the police. The vehicles of the Serbian journalists screeched away. We quickly extinguished the camera lights and disconnected the live TV link.

We all left the balcony and hid in the apartment. We were aware that any organisations from countries which had recognised Kosovo's independence, and individuals working for those organisations, were potential targets for the roaming gangs outside. We also realised that there was only one way in and out of the building. We hoped that they had not seen our lights and cameras.

For forty-five minutes we listened to the chanting and violence outside. But no one appeared to have noticed where we were. Eventually, I glanced out of the window to see ranks of police in full riot gear being deployed around the square. The threat was over.

When I walked out of the building, the streets were strewn with stones and rubbish. Burglar alarms were ringing from shops whose windows had been smashed. Nervous police officers were stationed at street corners. The smell of smoke and tear gas drifted down the street.

For nearly an hour there had been a total security vacuum in the centre of Belgrade. Why this was the case remained a mystery. But what it had clearly demonstrated was the power of the nationalists in Belgrade. They could – or they were allowed to – simply run amok through the centre of the capital. They had even been able to storm the United States Embassy. Tadić had won the election but the reformers were clearly not in total charge.

In December 2007 The Hague's Chief Prosecutor, Carla Del Ponte had left office. In a farewell news conference she said the fact that Karadžić and Mladić were still free was a 'stain' on the 'great achievements' of the Tribunal, and that she was very disappointed by this. She also strongly recommended that the Tribunal remain open after 2010, when it was due to close. Her new position would be less controversial and lower profile, as Swiss Ambassador to Argentina.

Over the next few weeks the war criminals issue died down. Journalists were concentrating on the internal political developments within Serbia. There was speculation over who would be appointed to which post in the new government, and there was the never-ending issue of Kosovo. In fact, all this was just the calm before the storm.

12

Arrest

'We had information about some person who was going around Serbia, practising alternative medicine. After the arrest, he was brought here to the Special Court. He spoke in a low voice giving the impression to some people that he was some kind of guru. He asked to be shaven and have his hair cut. I saw him the next day. He had turned back into his old self' – Vladimir Vukčević, Serbia's Chief War Crimes Prosecutor

I was at home watching a DVD of *American Gangster* when I noticed my muted mobile phone flashing in the dark. I put the film on hold and went over to the phone. It was a text message from my cousin in London. 'Have you seen the Karadžić capture chaos?' My heart lurched. Immediately I logged on to my computer and checked the news. It was true. Officials in Belgrade had announced that Radovan Karadžić had been arrested and was already in the custody of the Special War Crimes Court in the Serbian capital. I was stunned.

Three months previously I had taken a sabbatical from my career and was now living in Pristina in Kosovo. It seemed that timing was never going to be one of my strong points! I sat with my head in my hands, devastated that I had not been in Belgrade to witness the arrest. Already, I heard, there were street celebrations in Sarajevo, while in Belgrade, extra police had been deployed in case of unrest.

It turned out that Karadžić had been hiding under the

assumed name of Dragan David Dabić. He had been practising alternative medicine, treating patients, even attending
conferences and making speeches. It was incredible – and the
fact that his daughter Sonja had also been involved in setting
up an alternative medicine clinic in Pale did not escape me.

Karadžić had grown an enormous grey-white beard and
moustache and sported a pony-tail. A big pair of brown-
framed glasses completed the change of image. Despite his
otherwise familiar features and voice which had dominated
the world news during the 1990s, apparently nobody had
guessed his true identity. The Chief War Crimes Prosecutor
in Belgrade, Vladimir Vukčević, said that even he did not
recognise Karadžić when he was brought into court and
was standing just a few metres away. It seemed Karadžić,
alias Dabić, had been confident enough to set up his own
website. He was not only offering his own alternative health
treatments but selling a whole range of products related to
bio-energy healing.

More than 10,000 supporters of the former Bosnian Serb
President took to the streets. Many had been bussed in from
around the country. Violence broke out. Several people were
injured as riot police fired rubber bullets and tear gas and
protesters threw flares and rocks. City-centre shops had their
windows smashed. Debris littered the streets. Nationalist politicians condemned the arrest and described the government as
'treacherous'.

There could hardly have been a greater contrast than
Sarajevo where there were spontaneous street celebrations.

'I don't think there is jubilation,' said Haris Silajdžić,
Chairman of the Bosnian Presidency, who had helped negotiate Dayton on behalf of the Bosnian Government. 'But there
is relief because they waited too long – which was a disgrace
for the international community, for the war of justice, and
of course for Serbia,' he added.

Ljiljana Karadžić was more philosophical. 'When the phone
rang, I knew something was wrong. I'm shocked, confused.
At least now we know he is alive,' she said.

'I cried with happiness,' said Nidzara Ahmetasević, 34, interviewed in the *Independent*, who as a teenager was wounded during the shelling of Sarajevo. 'We just believed they would always remain at large and never be punished. Today, for the first time, I really feel like the war has ended.'

While he was in jail, Karadžić received visits from his brother Luka and Metropolitan Amfilohjie. Finally, a week after his capture, in a carefully co-ordinated operation during the night, he was driven from the court under armed guard, taken to a plane and flown to The Hague. The next day he made his first appearance in court. His beard and thick grey-white hair had been shorn. He was now easily recognisable as the figure who had appeared on TV screens around the world during the early-1990s. He was dressed in a smart suit and seemed composed, relaxed; he even made jokes about having an 'invisible adviser', referring perhaps to God. He confirmed his name and the last address he had stayed at while in hiding in Belgrade: Jurija Gagarina (Yuri Gagarin) Street, number 267. Asked where he was from, he said: 'I consider myself to be a national of Bosnia and Herzegovina, Republika Srpska, Montenegro, and Serbia.'

Karadžić declared that he did not want to have the indictment against him read out in full but would rather listen to the new amended version that was being prepared.

Evidently, the judge was not aware of this document, but its existence was confirmed by the Chief Prosecutor. Karadžić went on to make the claim that he had made a deal with the American negotiator, Richard Holbrooke, and that was the reason he had remained at liberty. But he produced no proof of any such agreement. He then said that he would have come to the court earlier but had feared for his life because of the delicate nature of the deal:

I want to show why I'm appearing before this court only now rather than in 1996, 1997, or 1998, when I had the intention of appearing here, but at that time I was in danger of being liquidated.

Later, in a written submission to the court, Karadžić expanded on these claims. He said that in 1996 Holbrooke 'made the statesmen and ministers who were my authorised representatives an offer'. This offer was the familiar 'deal' , the details of which were already widely familiar. He continued:

> I fulfilled my side of the agreement on the first day and I kept it for a very long time. I was careful how I moved about in the first few months after I had put the agreement with the USA into effect, not because of the international forces, whom I used to pass quietly and without demonstration, but because of possible adventurers and glory hunters. However, our intelligence services noted many aggressive activities by international forces in places from which I had just departed ... the intention to liquidate me was more than obvious.

Back in court, sensationally, Karadžić claimed that he had not actually been arrested on Monday 21 July 2008, as stated by the authorities in Belgrade, but on Friday 18 July, three days previously.

> For three days I was kidnapped by civilians whose identity I ignored. I was kept in place that I also ignored. My rights were not told me. I had no right for a telephone – to a telephone call or even a text message to my friends, lest they search for me in hospitals and morgues. And only after three days I was turned over to the special court, after which all the proceedings that followed were regular.

And those present were invited to draw a further inference:

> I must say that this is a matter of life and death. If Mr Holbrooke still wants my death and regrets that there is no death sentence here, I wonder if his arm is long enough to reach me here.

Radovan Karadžić's first appearance in court made quite an impact.

* * *

The Serbian policeman dozed in the passenger seat next to me, his snores starting to drown out the music on my car radio. He had also taken his shoes off. It was early in the morning and I was driving through southern Serbia on my way to Belgrade.

There had been a long tailback at the border and I had seen the policeman wandering along the lengthy line of cars. I tried not to catch his eye but he decided to knock on my window anyway, then asked if I was driving north and, if so, could I give him a lift? His night shift had just finished and he was hitch-hiking back home. Saying no was not really an option. He then added he would be able to take us to the front of the queue if I accepted. This seemed like a fair deal. I shifted my half-eaten sandwiches and water bottle to the back seat and in he got. Within five minutes he was asleep. Fifty miles further on, near the next big town, he woke up and we parted company.

I arrived in Belgrade in the middle of rush hour traffic. Around ten o'clock I reached the northern fringe of the city. The road in front was long and straight, like an arrow, heading for the suburb of Batajnica and my destination.

Beside the road was a disused blue police box, an old checkpoint which was now covered in ragged political posters and graffiti. There were a few houses nearby and beyond these fields stretched into the distance. This apparently was the place where Radovan Karadžić's years of freedom finally came to an end. He had been travelling on a number 73 bus from Belgrade to Batajnica on 21 July when Serbian intelligence agents pulled the bus over and identified him. Or that, at least, was the official version of events.

My cell phone rang. It was Marko. I had asked him to set up interviews with some people I hoped could shed a little more light on events surrounding the arrest. He had good news: Serbia's Chief War Crimes Prosecutor, Vladimir Vukčević, had agreed to see me.

I met Vukčević in his office. I had never seen him so relaxed. His was, after all, a very sensitive job, involving considerable personal risk. The assassination of Zoran Djindjic five years previously had shown that no one was immune from the reach of extremists and Vukčević had received his own fair share of death threats over the years. He ordered us orange juice and, after the initial pleasantries, told me about recent events.

'I found out about Karadžić on the sixteenth of June. Before that we had information about some person who was practising alternative medicine, going around Serbia, and also information that that person could be Radovan Karadžić. Of course, I had my reservations about it because we had a lot of information, although concerning Radovan Karadžić we had the least information . . . even Carla Del Ponte said she didn't know where he was, as though he had been swallowed by the earth . . . On the sixteenth of June I definitely found out that that person was most probably Karadžić . . . ninety-nine per cent certain.'

'If you knew that he was there on the sixteenth, why didn't you arrest him on the seventeenth?' I asked.

'These are operational details. It was not in our interests. We kept an eye on him and there was no need to hurry.'

I pressed him on how they finally identified Dragan Dabić as the real Radovan Karadžić. But he would not go into any detail apart from suggesting that a phone call had been intercepted which had helped lead to his eventual capture. I then asked about the precise timing of the arrest. The authorities claimed it had taken place on the Monday, but in court and via his lawyers Karadžić himself insisted he had been arrested the previous Friday.

'That's not important now. I did not arrest him. When he was arrested, I was informed by the security services. I don't have a reason not to believe them. I was informed on Monday. We were arranging how to bring him here, as there were protests, so we had to secure our building.'

'I know you were told that he was arrested on Monday. But do you actually believe that?'

'I don't have a reason not to believe it. That is totally irrelevant as this is a man whom we chased for fourteen years, and it doesn't matter if it was two days earlier or later.'

I asked him when he believed Karadžić had come to Belgrade.

'I don't know exactly, but he had been here for some time. He changed locations, moved flats, only two or three people knew his real identity. There is one curious detail: one of his neighbours in Yuri Gagarin Street works for Interpol. Every morning he would say to her, 'Good morning, madam,' and she would say, 'Good morning, neighbour.' In 2001 he was moving around with virtual freedom . . . even up until 2002. Ratko Mladić as well. The turning point was when Slobodan Milošević was arrested. That was when they really started to hide. Until then, they were completely free.'

But Vukčević would not say where Radavan Karadžić had travelled to exactly or who had been protecting him.

'We have a lot of information,' he said. 'We have a whole novel . . . with lots of false information. We even had reports that he was dead and testimonies from people who said they were at the funeral.'

Time was passing. It was clear I was not going to get any more hard facts from the Chief Prosecutor. Even if he knew them, he was not going to tell me.

When Karadžić was arrested his ID card said he was called Dragan Dabić. But who was the real Dabić and why had his name been chosen? Initial reports suggested that the original Dragan Dabić had been killed in Sarajevo during the war, but later it emerged that Karadžić's new identity was based on another Dragan Dabić who actually lived an hour's drive from the capital in a sleepy provincial town called Ruma. I took my faithful fixer Marko and headed out to find him.

Dragan Dabić's modest brown-painted house was at the end of an unremarkable street lined with trees. When we arrived no one was at home although the front door stood open. A neighbour told us that they did not know where Dabić himself was, but that his wife worked in the kitchen of the local school. We drove there and Mrs Dabić, by now familiar with the importunate demands of journalists, kindly gave us directions to a house where her husband was working.

I recognised him immediately from the photographs that had already appeared in the media. He was building a driveway with three other men. So this was the real Dragan Dabić. The former construction worker in his mid-sixties was not particularly happy to see me.

A couple of years older than Karadžić, Dragan Dabić could hardly have had a more different background from the man who had borrowed his identity. He had rarely been abroad, did not own a computer or even a mobile phone, and his hobbies included growing tomatoes in his garden and making brandy. He was wearing old Yugoslav Army camouflage trousers – very common in Serbia, especially among farmers and manual workers – and a blue shirt. He was a lot smaller than Karadžić, with short grey hair and a drooping Mexican-style moustache. The only thing the two men had in common were big brown-framed spectacles such as Karadžić had worn during his masquerade as an alternative healer.

Marko engaged Dabić in some banter while one of his workmates kept shouting 'Doctor' and laughing. Apparently, this was his new nickname around town. Dabić said he could not understand why Karadžić had borrowed his identity and added that he was considering suing the authorities. It was not clear why exactly he wanted to sue or on what grounds. Then there was another shout from his workmates. 'Hey, Doctor, come on. Time to get back to work!'

On my way back to Belgrade, I reflected on Dabić's anonymous, ordinary life and how it had made him such a perfect choice when building a new identity. It would be good to learn for how long Karadžić had been using that identity and who exactly had given him all the details.

The Luda Kuća (or Mad House) was situated on the outskirts of New Belgrade. The area is a sea of anonymous tower blocks stretching as far as the eye can see. The wide streets are set in a grid pattern criss-crossed by tram and bus routes. On the very outskirts of this area is Yuri Gagarin Street, the place where Karadžić had been living at the time of his arrest. His third-floor flat overlooked a small park and children's playground. The building was relatively modern and in better condition than many others in this part of town. It was a pleasant enough place – certainly preferable to the caves or forests of south-east Bosnia where many people, had presumed the former Bosnian Serb leader had been living. A few hundred metres from his flat was a small one-storey building. It had been a takeaway food outlet but, a few years previously, was turned into a small bar and given the name Luda Kuća. It was one of the very few locations the media knew that Karadžić had sometimes visited.

I parked the car and Marko and I headed over to the Mad House. It was early-afternoon and the sun was out. Clearly, this place was never going to win any awards for architecture or design. It was one of those small, smoky dives frequented by pensionable men who liked to sit and play cards and make their drinks last. But the Luda did at least make a bit of an effort, with a few broken chairs set outside under the trees.

Marko was not sure we would be too welcome. In fact, a journalist colleague had been chased out of the bar a few days earlier, after getting into a political discussion with the locals. Marko told me to wait outside while he made a couple of phone calls. Ten minutes later an ancient Mercedes pulled up and two well-built men got out. They were our insurance policy should things get out of hand.

I followed them inside. There were three or four tables with half a dozen or so people sitting at them, playing cards and drinking beer. We sat down near the door. Silence descended. After the barman took our orders, one of my new companions started up a conversation with some men at the next table. I glanced around the room. One bottle of Scotch whisky sat on a shelf above the bar beside various kinds of *rakia*, but it was the pictures on the walls that grabbed my attention. There were two separate pictures of Karadžić and Mladić and, to our right, a painting of Karadžić – hastily produced since the arrest and showing him in his thick, grey beard. I later learned it was hanging above what had been Karadžić's customary seat.

It emerged that he had first come into the bar just over a year ago and had become a regular customer, sometimes stopping off at the Mad House after visiting the grocery shop opposite. He'd been seen a few times chatting to someone who was known as 'the Captain' because of the military-style hat he sometimes wore. His picture also featured on one of the yellow-painted walls. The Captain was wearing a white military uniform and a big smile. We managed to persuade someone to give us his telephone number.

As we prepared to leave I noticed another photograph on the wall, close to the painting of the bearded Dabić. It looked remarkably like the village of Petnica in Montenegro, birthplace of Karadžić. I asked the barman.

'Oh, no . . . it's not,' he said. 'But it's very close to Petnica. In fact, it's the next village. It's called Poscenje, the home village of the owner of Luda Kuća.'

What were the chances, I wondered, that Karadžić and the owner of Luda Kuća were from adjacent villages? It seemed an incredible coincidence. Perhaps Karadžić had spotted the picture the first time he had come into the bar and that had been a good enough reason for him to make it his regular.

The next day I visited the offices of lawyer Goran Petronijević who was acting on Karadžić's behalf. Bald-headed and confident, he talked in an upbeat way about the forthcoming trial. He did not wish to speculate on the way his client had been apprehended but it was clear he had his own ideas and betrayal figured among them. He said his client had no case to answer for Srebrenica. To prove his point, he produced two books highlighting the way that Serbs had suffered there. One even had a list of the Serb dead. He said the number of Muslim dead had been exaggerated. He agreed to see if it might be possible for me to meet and interview his client, but did not think the court in The Hague would allow it.

*　　*　　*

An autumn downpour was thrashing into the swirling waters of the Danube. Thick grey clouds hung low over the river, obscuring its opposite bank. I was warm and dry and getting hungry in a comfortable riverside restaurant, waiting for a contact I had never met before. It was gone four o'clock.

Suddenly, the doors opened and a man wearing a short-sleeved blue shirt arrived, carrying a little bag under his arm. He peered round the restaurant and I stood up and made myself known. He joined me at the table and sat down, placing his bag and car keys to one side. We both ordered fish, and then it was straight down to business. I was well aware that he was taking a risk by talking to me. He had worked for one of the Serbian intelligence agencies and had had access to highly confidential information.

'I am one hundred per cent certain,' he said, 'that Karadžić was arrested on Friday the eighteenth in the evening. He was on a bus on the way to Batajnica. There were around a dozen passengers, including undercover intelligence officers. On the outskirts of the town, the bus was stopped. [The man known as] Dabić was sitting near the front of the bus and wearing a hat. He was asked to get off. There was no trouble, no argument. He was put in a car and driven back to Belgrade. During the next few days around five of those passengers rang in to report what they had seen. The driver was ordered to take a thirty-day holiday in Bosnia, to keep him out of the public eye.'

'Where was Karadžić taken?'

'To BIA (Bezbednosno Informativna Agencija, or the Serbian Security Information Agency) headquarters, opposite the military hospital. He was blindfolded before going into the grounds. He was held for two days and questioned. Agents went through the stuff he was carrying, including his laptop and the discs he had with it. Some of those discs were destroyed in order to cover up any incriminating connections. DNA tests were also carried out to confirm his identity. A few days later, whatever was left was put in a different bag and dumped by the roadside, close to where the arrest had taken place. The Chief War Crimes Prosecutor, Vukčević, was eventually informed of the arrest and he [Karadžić] was handed over to the court on the Monday.'

'Where was he headed at the time of the arrest?'

The waiter arrived at the table, bringing our fish. I had ordered a glass of wine, my companion only water.

'It's believed he had been tipped off that he was being followed and was making a run for it. The idea was that he was going to meet a contact in Batajnica and then be driven back to Belgrade in order to try and lose his pursuers. Then he was going to travel to Croatia – to Split, in fact.'

'Who tipped him off?'

'He was being protected by certain people within the intelligence and political structures. But with the changing political environment, there was concern that Karadžić's identity could soon be discovered, so they tried to help him get away. But he was already being followed by other members of the intelligence services. In fact, he had been under twenty-four-hour surveillance for the previous month.'

My lunch companion had highlighted one of the key changes in Serbia during the previous year. In February 2008, the pro-European and reformist President Boris Tadić had been re-elected with 51 per cent of the vote, narrowly defeating the hard-line nationalist, Tomislav Nikolić, from the Serbian Radical party. The Radical Party's leader, Vojislav Šešelj, was himself facing trial in The Hague on war crimes charges.

Then, in May 2008, Serbia held a General Election. Tadić's pro-European bloc received the largest number of votes, but not enough to form a government outright. Two months of coalition talks took place, with Serbia poised on a knife edge between a pro-European government or a nationalist-orientated government espousing closer ties with Russia. In one of the classic ironies of Balkan politics, Milošević's old socialists threw in their lot with Tadić, and the die was cast.

Crucially, the division of cabinet posts left the pro-Europeans with the posts of Prime Minister, Foreign Minister, Defence Minister, Justice Minister, and the right to select the head of the intelligence service, BIA. Tadić had gradually consolidated his position. It was to be a real turning point for Serbia – and for the fortunes of Radovan Karadžić.

My contact claimed that Milošević had decided in 1999 to hand false IDs to some people. Karadžić had been one beneficiary, he maintained, but would not elaborate further. It was the new personnel within BIA who had started to ask the crucial questions about surveillance operations which led to the discovery of Karadžić's whereabouts. The BIA was internally divided. Some of the new intake questioned whether various 'surveillance' operations were in fact covert monitoring and protection of subjects by the old guard. When one particular 'subject' came under closer scrutiny, Karadžić was identified and arrested. Apparently, the reason why some of the discs that Karadžić was carrying in the bag when he was arrested were destroyed, was because they would have revealed the connections that Karadžić had with BIA. They discovered he was being protected or monitored by the old guard within the agency. This could have proved embarrassing for everyone.

The sky was beginning to clear over the Danube and I was getting a much clearer picture of Karadžić's last days at large. But I still had no positive proof and did not know if I could trust my new source. Then I remembered the Captain.

13

The Fugitive

'As the bearded New Age healer Dragan Dabić, he became a regular at the little pub on the high-rise estate where he was soon giving virtuoso performances on a lute-like instrument, playing beneath a portrait of himself hung above the bar' – *The Times*, 24 July 2008

He was waiting for us on a street corner not far from his apartment. As agreed, the Captain was carrying a newspaper under his arm so that we would recognise him. He had given us directions to where he lived on the other side of Belgrade. We had journeyed through the rush-hour traffic, passing the military hospital and BIA headquarters. The Captain guided us to a parking space, then, after firm handshakes, led us up to his flat. He might have been 70 years old but he looked much younger. He sat us down in comfortable armchairs and disappeared into the kitchen, returning a few moments later with two glasses and a bottle of orange juice.

He told us he was a retired railway engineer and had been a regular down at the Luda Kuća bar. He said he visited that part of town because it was near the River Sava where he liked to go for a walk. He'd spent a lot of time in that area with his family and friends when he was younger, and even produced a photo album to prove it. Luda Kuća was at the end of the tram route, a perfect place for getting away from the hustle and bustle of city life and chatting and drinking with friends. I asked him when he had first met Dr Dragan Dabić.

'I met him a few times before his arrest. The first time was very brief and we did not really talk. It was three or four months before his arrest. The second time we talked for more than an hour.'

'How was he dressed?'

'He was wearing black trousers, a white shirt and white hat. Everything was white on his head. We got into a discussion about a friend of mine who had psychological problems. Dabić said he was a psychiatrist and offered to help. I told him that she was depressed and had been undergoing treatment. He was polite and asked what medicines she had been taking and when she had been in hospital. After that he told me that he'd got his own practice should I need help. He said I could contact him if needed. He gave me his card. I gave him mine. On that occasion we were talking for about one and a half hours. He was a very nice person. He offered his help to a patient although he had no obligation to do that.'

'What else do you remember?'

'I saw him perhaps half a dozen times. I remember he never wanted to talk about politics, it was just small talk about the drinks or the bar. I don't like talking about politics either because people start arguing immediately. I saw him a few times at the little grocery shop next to Luda Kuća. He used to go there about five o'clock in the afternoon. He had his cotton carrier bag. I remember he always seemed to be wearing black and white clothes. He was very noticeable in that black and white combination, with that beard and hair of his. I used to say to him, "Good day, Doctor." He was always alone. I never saw him with another person. People in the bar said he enjoyed a glass of red wine but, honestly, I cannot remember that.'

'How did you hear about his real identity?'

'The owner of Luda Kuća rang me up to tell me. I watched television and could not believe it at first. Nobody at Luda Kuća could have guessed that that was Radovan Karadžić. He was a decent man, though.'

Before we left, the Captain proudly showed me the business card that Karadžić had given him. It advertised an alternative health clinic and listed its services. There was an address on it. I slipped it into my back pocket.

I had made an appointment to meet Radovan Karadžić's guru, the man who had trained the former Bosnian Serb President in bio-energy healing. According to a number of reports, this man had known Karadžić alias Dabić for a number of years. He lived in an anonymous street, not easy to find, on the outskirts of Belgrade. The house was sandwiched between the tower blocks that dominated the area but, on arrival, I was pleasantly surprised to see it set in a garden bursting with flowers. I walked up to the front door and rang the bell. I heard footsteps approaching slowly. There was the twist of a key and then the door swung open.

Mina Minić had clear blue serene eyes and a huge white beard, immediately reminiscent of Karadžić's when he was found. We shook hands and he led me down a few steps to a separate entrance. This was his work studio: a cramped room with a plethora of items spread around the room. He sat behind a desk and leaned back in his chair. I sat down opposite him on a bench next to a stack of shelves.

'That is exactly where Radovan sat,' Minić told me with a distinct tone of pride in his voice. As Marko chatted with him, I glanced around this Aladdin's cave of bric-à-brac. On the walls hung various photographs and pictures: from what seemed to be the Second World War, family photographs and some Serbian religious images plus a wall calendar from 2005. There was a board full of certificates, a little library of books, and what looked like a cooker next to the chair in which Minić was sitting. On the tables were a number of water bottles. I noticed a *gusla* propped up in the corner.

Minić pointed out a book about Karadžić which had been sent to him by the former President's supporters, thanking him for the help he had given him. But it was some peculiar metal rings that held my attention. Each one contained a number of circular metal tubes, attached to each other at different angles. It was like being in some mad inventor's studio.

Mina Minić was a self-styled guru of alternative medicine, specialising in bio-energy. He would have remained well off the international radar screen if he had not somehow become a friend and colleague of Europe's most wanted man. But before I could begin my questions he fired a few at me, asking my name, where I came from, whether I had religion, whether I was a Communist. Seemingly satisfied with my answers, he fell silent for a moment. I took the opportunity to ask how he had first come across Dragan Dabić.

'It was spring 2005. I had just returned from a conference in Moscow. He came here unannounced. He met my wife, gave her a bunch of flowers, kissed her hand and asked for me. My wife told him I was here and brought him down. He sat where you are now. He looked like he was in trouble . . . you know, a bit scruffy. He looked like a priest. He said he wanted to check his health using my method of *radiostezija*. I told him it cost thirty Euros which he paid immediately. Would you like me to do the same on you that I did on him?'

I gave my assent and Minić immediately picked up a piece of string with what looked like two metal weights on either end. It was called a *visak* (or plumb line). He dangled one end over a chart of numbers and figures and let it swing like a pendulum. He held the other end in his hand and pointed at me. He then went through a whole series of assessments relating to my circulation, heart condition, energy levels, mental state, spirituality, etc. He pronounced that I was in very good health although I should eat more water melons for my kidneys. He also said I had reached 'genius' level on the mental test and that, if I wished, I had the potential to become an alternative medicine practitioner myself. If I passed his €400 five-day course, I could start straight away. I made no commitment and returned to my interview.

Minić confirmed that Karadžić had taken this same course, paying the €400 straight away. He had passed easily. Over time, the two men grew closer and Minić gave his new friend the nickname 'David', a shortened form of the Serbian words *'da vidim'* which means 'let me see'. Apparently, Karadžić had an insatiable appetite for learning and was always keen to see new methods and techniques. He thus became known as Dragan David Dabić. Eventually Minić gave him a set of keys to the studio and told him that he could use it whenever he wanted. Attached to the studio was a small bedroom and bathroom that Dabić was also able to use. 'There was an open door for him,' Minić told me. 'He came and went as he liked. I did not always know whether he was here or not.'

'What did he tell you about where he had come from?'

'He told me that he had arrived from the United States, from New York, and that he would one day go back there and use the skills that I was teaching him. He said his family were abroad and that he received a foreign pension. Later, I found out he was a psychiatrist and also that he worked with some writers and poets. He was helping me edit a book.' Karadžić also told Minić he had a wife called Ljiljana and children named Sonja and Sasa – which was all true. But his claim that he was a Bosnian Croat and that he had graduated in medicine from Zagreb University was not. He always carried a laptop with him and, during his tuition by Minić, noted everything on to the computer. He also carried four or five mobile phones and sometimes spoke in English on them.

'He told me he went one day to Sveti Marko's [Saint Mark's] church in the centre of Belgrade to light a candle. He put his bag on a table. The bag contained his *visaks*, mobile phones, documents and so on. After lighting his candle, when he turned back, his bag had disappeared. Someone had stolen it.'

'What did you think about him?'

'Radovan is the greatest genius of all time who could help a man. In the next moment he might go crazy and do terrible things. I feel I must defend him. Whatever he did, he did in temper. When his loved ones are threatened or killed . . . then he snaps. He avenges those that were killed. I see him as a commander who was constantly in this situation.'

Before I left, Minić suddenly said he would see if he could contact Karadžić in The Hague, using his *visak*. I was sceptical but polite. A moment later, with a totally straight face, he told me, 'Radovan doesn't object to this interview. He supports you. I am receiving the best feedback now. I ask Radovan now if he's happy that we are doing this and he is saying yes. One hundred per cent, yes.'

I was thinking about the timing of the events Minić had just outlined. According to him, Karadžić arrived at his house in the spring of 2005, already wearing his thick white beard. A beard like that would take at least a year to grow so it was clear that, wherever Karadžić was before, he'd been bearded since at least 2004 – an important factor when analysing alleged sightings of the former Bosnian Serb President. But Minić did not seem to know any more about his friend's past. All I had learned was that Karadžić had been in Belgrade since at least 2005, and had had a beard since 2004.

As we drove away from Minić's house I took out the business card the Captain had given me, advertising Dabić's alternative healing company. On the back was a list of the services offered and on the front an address and telephone number. I got Marko to ring it and, surprisingly, the phone was answered. The person on the other end of the line agreed to meet me. We arranged to rendezvous two days later in a cafe near the main market in New Belgrade.

Predrag was in his mid-thirties, with intelligent eyes and short hair. He was quite happy to talk and told me he had met Dragan Dabić back in 2006, when he had come to Predrag's health food stall at the nearby market. Over the following weeks Dabić was a regular customer and they had become friends.

'We eventually decided to set up a business together. We actually registered it in the winter of 2007. He said he was a psychiatrist and was trained in bio-energy healing. Between us we thought we could make some money. We got on very well. We tried to promote the business through the various seminars he attended.'

'Did you have no suspicions at all about who he really was?'

'No, he struck me as a very intelligent man and I could see people liked him. But I had no idea who he really was.'

It seemed amazing. Karadžić was so confident of his disguise he was not only seeing patients and appearing at alternative health seminars, he was actively involved in setting up a business partnership.

They were sitting at a large round table. I was late and most of the food was gone. An expensive bottle of red, rather than white, wine was standing in an ice bucket next to the table, and I was immediately offered a drink. I had come to this restaurant to catch up with Marko, not realising he would have company. There were two other people at the table with him who welcomed me like a long-lost friend. Conversation shifted from talk of international travel to the recent riots in Belgrade where the United States Embassy had been stormed and burnt by protestors opposed to US recognition of an independent Kosovo. We then got on to the Karadžić story. I mentioned I was trying to find out where he had worked and lived while he was on the run.

'Why don't you try that clinic on the outskirts? I am sure he used to work there,' said the older of the two men.

'Oh, really? What's it called?'

'I think it's called Nova Vita,' the other man put in.

Marko made a couple of calls and everything was arranged.

Still not knowing with whom I had been talking for the past 45 minutes, I stood up with Marko and said goodbye to our two companions. I was given a hug, the traditional Serbian triple kiss and a pat on the back. As we neared the door, I asked Marko out of the corner of my mouth: 'Perhaps you could tell me now who they were.'

'The older guy used to be one of the leading figures in the Serbian underworld. Very closely associated with Milošević. Famous in the nineties for one of his cigarette businesses. You know, when the sanctions were on.'

'Well . . . that's just great Marko. Thanks for the heads up!'

* * *

The Nova Vita clinic sat in the lee of a hill in a thickly forested suburb of Belgrade. Taking the main road from the city centre, you first passed the Rakovica Monastery and immediately behind that was Nova Vita (or New Life). The clinic boasted up-to-date facilities and equipment and treated anyone who could afford its fees, including people from overseas who travelled there for the specialist treatments they offered. A variety of alternative remedies and methods were applied. Its website claimed to 'provide high standards of health care, that is, the application of the latest medical technology in the treatment of malignant and chronic internal diseases'.

After some initial reluctance to speak to me, the manager confirmed that Dabić had visited the clinic often and offered to help out. He had apparently told them he was a doctor from Sarajevo who believed that psychotherapy was an important tool in the treatment of cancer patients. Although he'd been keen to work at the hospital, the manager told him it was not possible. But he could often be seen talking to the patients, sometimes in English. He seemed to be living with absolutely no fear of discovery or arrest.

On our way out of the hospital, a man asked us if he could have a private word. I was led into a small alcove and in hushed tones told me I should contact a man in Banja Luka in Bosnia who could tell me a lot more about Dragan Dabić. Having passed on the telephone number, my informant did not hang around, but made off rapidly down the hospital corridor.

I returned to Sarajevo and, in the days that followed, established that this new contact ran his own health food business and had met Dragan Dabić on a number of occasions. His name was Vojislav Dudurović. He agreed to meet me. During this preparatory conversation he told me that not only had he met Dabić in Belgrade, he had even spent several nights in his flat in Yuri Gagarin Street.

I had covered thousands of kilometres journeying around the former Yugoslavia on the trail of Radovan Karadžić but this was the first time I had gone to Banja Luka. The town's non-Serbian population had been almost entirely forced from the city during the war. Some had been killed, others detained in the infamous prison camps nearby. The lucky ones had escaped in the very early days or been forcibly evicted and made to flee to Government-controlled territory.

Banja Luka is a pretty town with tree-lined streets and open-air cafes. The River Vrbas which passes through it is a popular swimming venue in summer. Like most places it was suffering economically but its location in the north of the country, close to the Croatian border, put it in a good position to benefit from trade with the country's neighbours.

Vojislav Dudurović was 74 but had the firm handshake of a man in his twenties. His jacket was too loose for his lean body and he liked to laugh loud and uproariously, especially if the joke was risqué. We followed him to his health food factory in the village where he was born. As we arrived he pointed out the house where Croatian fascist, Ustasha, had murdered his mother in World War Two. There are few places in Bosnia where there is not some such bloody history to recite. His factory consisted mainly of a large warehouse containing shelves and shelves of jars and packets stuffed with health products, most seemingly derived from chestnuts. We sat down at a long table and he offered us some apple juice and chestnut cake. I asked him when he had first met Dragan Dabić.

'It was a couple of years ago at the Innovation Fair in Belgrade in the National Museum. I was exhibiting there. Actually it was some equipment for processing chestnuts. Dabić also was exhibiting. He was using the *visak*, doing health checks on people and also showing them how to water divine. I thought he looked like a priest or a saint. I walked up to him and he introduced himself as Dragan Dabić with an "artistic" name [nickname] of David.'

'Why did you think he looked like a saint?'

'With his white beard and moustache and part of his hair tied back, he could have been in one of those frescoes of the saints. He also looked very serious. Saints are not jokers or *bon vivants* like the rest of us. The next day, we actually bumped into each other in the main Post Office in Belgrade and that's when we had a longer conversation. At the end, he said if I ever needed a place, I could stay at his. I took his offer up and over the next couple of years I must have been about fifteen to twenty times to his flat in Yuri Gagarin Street.'

'Describe his place.'

'It was on the third floor of a tower block. Quite a small flat, with only one bedroom which I never saw. As you entered, the kitchen was on the left and the bathroom on the right. If you carried straight on down the hallway you came into the lounge which had a couple of sofa beds. He told me that one of them was mine and I was always welcome to sleep there. There was a big library which he said belonged to the owner. There were a few paintings, including some religious icons. I did not see any photographs. There was a table, a couple of chairs, and always some nibbles like almonds, dates, walnuts, dried fruit, raisins . . . those kind of things. He drank all sorts of teas. He taught me how to make them properly: after the water boils you wait three minutes and then you pour it over the tea leaves. He claimed that by preparing tea this way you get the most benefit from it.'

'What was he like? What did you talk about?'

'He was a very serious man. Very rarely had a smile on his face. We mostly talked about bio-energy and healing. He said he treated a lot of people in Belgrade and that he found it very tiring. He would go to people's homes, they didn't come to his. He liked to play the synthesiser in the evening in order to relax. We also exchanged views on nutrition. He never ate after six p.m. like me and always seemed very healthy. He seemed to be mentally very strong. I asked him why he had offered to let me sleep in his apartment, having known me for only two days. He told me that it was easy to recognise a friend. So, we connected somehow. There was bio-energy potential between us.'

'Where did he tell you he came from?'

'He told me that his family was living in America and that he lived there too, but he had come because he could make more money in this profession here than in America. The idea was that when his children had completed their studies he would buy a house and they'd all be together. He said he had a boy and a girl.'

Dudurović went over to one of the other tables. He came back with another version of his chestnut cake, which he cut into small pieces. He placed toothpicks in each piece so we could pick them up more easily. He told me that he had tried to get Dabić some work and had introduced him at an alternative medicine clinic called the Nova Vita on the outskirts of Belgrade.

'Had you ever met Karadžić before? For instance, during the Bosnian War.'

'There was one time in 1992, when I attended a meeting of businessmen. Karadžić was giving a speech in the cultural hall in Banja Luka. He was trying to gain support and said we only needed two hundred businessmen to lead the economy of Republika Srpska. He was staying at the Hotel Bosna and asked us to register our support for him.'

'Did you?'

'No, I was my own man.'

'When was the last time you saw Dragan Dabić?'

'At the end of May 2008. We went on a cruise on the Danube. I arrived the night before, about nine in the evening. He was with a woman called Mila. The next day we cruised for three hours around Kalemegdan Park. There were more than a hundred people on board. On the way back they brought out a big cake for everyone. But before we could eat it, everyone had to introduce themselves, give their name, where they were from, etc. When it was my turn, I said I was delighted to be there because I could feel the huge positive energy. I explained I had travelled from Banja Luka just to be present.'

'How did Dabić introduce himself?'

'Dragan David Dabić, psychiatrist. Mila said she was his friend. They were invited to cut the cake together. Then he graciously stepped forward, crossed himself, took the knife and, together with Mila, cut the cake. After the cruise I drove us all back to the flat. We had coffee and I came back to Banja Luka.'

'How do you feel now, knowing that Dragan Dabić was in fact Radovan Karadžić? Do you feel that you were deceived?'

'Not for one second did I imagine it was Radovan Karadžić. He disguised himself so well. No, I do not feel deceived personally. He had to conceal his identity to avoid being discovered.'

Dudurović's phone rang then. He apologised and said he would have to answer it. I ate some more of the cake which was extremely tasty even if I did not feel any surge in my biorhythms.

'Well, that's good news,' he said when he'd hung up. 'Last week I gave some of my medicine to a woman who complained that her husband could no longer make love to her because he had a bad back. Last night he took a dose and was able to make love to his wife for the first time in months. She just rang up to thank me. Ha, ha! Very good! Anyway, where were we?'

The conversation rambled on very pleasantly for some time. It was growing dark outside and I thought I had probably had enough chestnut cake for one day. Dudurović had given us a fascinating insight into the domestic existence of Dragan Dabić but I was still no wiser about how he had managed to evade his pursuers for a whole decade.

14

Revelation

'He enjoyed a glass of wine while he watched football. He
lived quite normally for years. He used to laugh at the latest
raid to find him. But towards the end, he felt the pressure.
He wanted to hold on just a little longer' – Anonymous

The orange candles burned steadily in the twilight. Only when
the door to the church opened did their flames dance in unison,
shadows magnified on the wall behind. Faded paintings of
Serbian saints and kings flickered in the half light, images from
the past still relevant today. Incense from an earlier ceremony
hung faintly in the air. It was early-morning and I had been
travelling most of the night, hoping I was not on another wild
goose chase. Then I heard footsteps outside, crunching over
the thin layer of snow that had fallen during the night, the
first of winter. The door creaked open and a silhouette was
outlined on the threshold.

The previous day, Marko had called me. We had not been in
touch for a couple of weeks. The trail had gone cold and, to
be honest, I did not know what to do next. The authorities
were not being any help and I felt I had exhausted most of
my other leads.

'Someone has got in touch.' Marko's voice sounded urgent.
'He wouldn't say how he found me or what he really wanted,
but he says he has the answers that you are looking for. If you
are ready, he'll meet you. But the meeting has to be tomorrow

and he does not have much time. It is quite a long drive for you and he wants to meet you at seven in the morning.' Marko gave me the name of a church, the village and its location. 'It's up to you. It could be a complete waste of time.'

He seemed a little nervous, glancing around the empty church. Before he reached me, the door behind him swung open again and another man came in. He stood still for a moment and then moved aside and leaned against the wall.

The first man reached me and we shook hands. He seemed to relax a little.

'It's good to meet you finally. Long journey?' He gave me no time to answer. 'Sorry this meeting had to be arranged so quickly, and I am sorry for all this cloak-and-dagger stuff, but it has to be this way.' His English was perfect, to the extent that I was not immediately sure whether or not it was his first language. In the half-light I could see he was around my age, maybe slightly older. His eyes were dark as was his hair. He was wearing a dark blue winter jacket and jeans. His manner was easy and confident but there was tension in the air nevertheless. He glanced over his shoulder towards the door and gave a quick nod to the other man.

'He with you?' I asked.

'Yes.'

'Why's he not joining us?'

'No reason. He travels with me.' I looked over his shoulder. His companion stood motionless, watching us.

'So, who are you?' I asked.

'It doesn't matter who I am. The important thing is that I can tell you a few things you might want to know.'

He took me by the elbow and started leading me to the far corner of the church. 'I think it is right that people should know these things.' I heard footsteps keeping pace with ours on the other side of the building.

We stood together under a window. Anyone else coming into the church would not have been able to see us unless they came close to where we were standing.

'I can't tell you who I am. It's not that I do not trust you
. . . in fact, I am telling you what I know *because* I trust you. It's
just that I have to protect certain people. In fact, I can't tell
you everything I know either. It's up to you.'

'You want money?'

'No. Look, do you want to hear what I have to say?'

I nodded.

He took a deep breath.

'When Radovan Karadžić left Pale in 1998, he came to
Belgrade. He was not running from cave to cave in Bosnia or
from monastery to monastery in Montenegro. He was not
criss-crossing the Bosnian, Serbian or Montenegrin borders
with an army of bodyguards. He did not go on holiday in
Croatia or practise alternative medicine in Austria or go and
visit literary friends in Russia. He stayed in Belgrade, right
under the noses of the authorities.'

He started to walk away from me, looking up at the frescoes
on the walls. 'Beautiful, aren't they?' He spoke without looking
at me. 'You know, they date back centuries. There's so much
history here.' He continued walking away and I followed. He
was speaking confidently and clearly; he certainly had the air
of someone who knew what he was talking about. I did not
want to interrupt his train of thought even though it seemed
to be drifting to other matters. For the next few minutes he
circled the church, pointing out various icons and translating
some of the old Serbian inscribed on the walls. I just listened,
uncomfortably conscious all the time of the other man, our
shadow.

'Milošević had originally offered him the opportunity of
staying at one of Tito's old villas near Belgrade but Karadžić
had refused. He made his own way to Belgrade and took a
team of bodyguards with him. They were provided by the
Bosnian Serb authorities. They looked after him and protected
him. For years.

'In the autumn of 2000, those guards were withdrawn. The
political climate had changed. The money had run out.
Questions were being asked and the pressure was becoming

too great. With the withdrawal of the official bodyguards, Karadžić decided to select his own team and paid them himself. It was quite a small group. They had to keep a low profile.'

The door to the church suddenly creaked open again. There was a gust of cold air. A monk wearing black robes walked slowly across the back of the church. I was suddenly aware that our shadow had interposed himself between us and the new arrival. In the dim light I caught a glimpse of him, eyes trained on the monk, who padded on, oblivious to our presence, into a side chapel.

'In 2003 or 2004,' my contact continued, 'pressure was mounting again. Karadžić became too hot to handle. So someone was selected to look after him. Just one person. Someone who had no connection with any of the other bodyguards, someone who had no criminal record, someone who was above reproach.'

'Who was that?'

'I wish I could tell you.'

'This is ridiculous,' I said.

The monk reappeared, carrying a small leather bag in one hand and a candle in the other. He was young, with light brown hair. He fumbled for a lighter, flicked it on and lit the candle before placing it in a metal holder along with some others. I could see him muttering a prayer.

'For the next four years,' my informant picked up the story, 'Karadžić continued to live in Belgrade. A sort of cordon sanitaire had been created around him. The idea was to sever links with everyone else, for his own safety. Except for this one man. It was during this period that he acquired the identity of Dragan Dabić.'

'How?'

'I cannot tell you. But it was not the Serbian state who gave it him – or any other official authority for that matter. To all intents and purposes it was a genuine identity card but, in fact, all the details were false except for the name and birth date of Dragan Dabić. The rest was pure fantasy.'

This was very much at odds with the details my informant at the fish restaurant had given me, but I stayed silent.

'The new identity gave Karadžić a new lease of life. For years he had been living anonymously in a series of apartments in Belgrade, not even going out for a walk. He was scared of his own shadow. But now he felt confident enough to move around, to start a new career ... as an alternative health practitioner.' My contact glanced at his watch.

'That is when he went to learn how to use the *visak* from Mina Minić, to set up the company, to go and drink and make friends in the Luda Kuća.'

There was a distant sound of classical music. At first I did not realise where it was coming from, then I saw my contact delve into one of the pockets of his blue jacket and pull out a mobile phone. He checked the caller before walking to another corner of the church. I noticed he had a slight limp.

'I have to go. Sorry.' He seemed genuinely apologetic. 'If you come back here tomorrow at the same time, I will tell you the rest.'

I did not feel there was any choice.

'Sure, yes, of course ... thank you,' I said.

He walked out of the door. A few seconds later, our shadow did the same.

There was only one hotel in the village but there was no problem about finding a room. The place had obviously seen better days. Its bright orange wallpaper was peeling at the corners and the clock hanging above the reception desk had stopped at half past three in the afternoon, in what year was anybody's guess. I was handed my key, attached to a lump of wood which could have doubled as a cosh. I was soon unpacking my travel bag and rinsing my tired face in a bowl of cold water. Afterwards, I went down to the restaurant and ordered a heavy duty Turkish coffee. The only food on offer was a cheese sandwich. Outside, snow was falling steadily. I was engulfed by a sense of overwhelming fatigue, but my mind was still racing with questions.

My first question was, why was I being given all this information in the first place? My contact had told me that he thought it was 'right that people knew these things'. But why was he telling me? I had probably written more stories about the Karadžić case and followed the developments closer than any other journalist, but was this a good enough reason to tell me these things? Why did he feel he could trust me? And then there were the more practical questions. Was it all true? Had Karadžić always lived in Belgrade? Had he not been hiding in Bosnia or Montenegro, spending years in a cave or a monastery? I had been told that his Dragan Dabić identity had been provided by the Milošević regime – so was I now to believe this was not true? That instead he had acquired the identity through his own private means, whatever they were? Had he not been protected by a well-armed group of bodyguards, at least not during the final few years, but rather by one individual who had no links to any security structure? Most of this went against the received wisdom of journalists, prosecutors and everyone else hunting Karadžić. Could I really believe what I was being told now? And why was I being told it at all, even if it were true?

I finished my coffee. The snow was coming down more heavily but I decided to take a walk nevertheless. The village was in a steep valley and, looking up, I could see thick forest shadowing the slopes. It could have been Switzerland.

My phone rang. It was Marko, wanting to see how things had gone. I gave him a brief resumé.

'Remember, try and test whatever he tells you. You have to be sure,' he said at the end. I hung up. I had a long day ahead.

The next morning there was no other car parked outside the church and I suspected I was first to arrive. But when I entered, my contact was already leaning against the far wall near the altar. It looked like he was texting someone on his mobile phone. As I neared him, he straightened up and slipped the phone into his pocket. He smiled and we shook hands. After some perfunctory remarks, he continued his story.

'Our friend not joining us?' I quipped.

'Over there.' He nodded. Standing a few metres behind the altar was our shadow. Without further ceremony, my informant launched back into his story.

'From one of the apartments he lived in, Karadžić even witnessed the NATO bombing during the Kosovo conflict in 1999. He kept on the move but virtually always in New Belgrade. With its expanding businesses and tower blocks, this was home for thousands of people who had moved to the city not only during the past few years but also during the sixties and seventies. The area did not have the roots and neighbourliness of the older part of Belgrade across the river. There was less chance of any neighbours becoming inquisitive or suspicious.'

'How did he rent his apartments?'

'Using the new name. He moved into his last apartment, the one in Yuri Gagarin Street, in the summer of 2007. By this time he had become quite accomplished with the *visak* and, coupled with his professional skills as a psychiatrist, had built up a base of patients. He worked at three or four clinics around Belgrade. And, as everyone knows, he even set up a website and began appearing at various seminars propounding his various theories and techniques.'

'How did he live in the months before he was arrested?'

'He was in good health. Lived a relatively normal life. He had a flute and a synthesiser. Watched football on television. I think his favourite teams were Belgrade Red Star and Manchester United. He used to go down to the local betting shop and chance his arm when the big European games were on. He enjoyed a glass of beer or wine, although only in moderation. And he looked after himself, eating health foods.

'Obviously, he was careful about his security. He had a number of mobile phones and, after a month or two, he would discard them and get new ones. He used to read newspapers a lot, especially *Politika*. He must have felt under constant pressure. We think he was waiting for the end of the year, for The

Hague Tribunal to close down, and then maybe he was going to hand himself over to the Serbian authorities.'

'Do you think his family knew where he was?'

'Some members, yes.'

'Who?'

'I cannot say.'

'Did the Serbian state or intelligence services know where he was?'

'Some within the service knew. But they did not know his location all the time. You must remember that opinion on Karadžić was split. Some believed him to be a hero, someone to be supported and helped. Others believed he should go to The Hague for the sake of Serbia and the Serbian people. There was that continual division.'

'Who knew?'

'I cannot say.'

'Who was protecting Radovan Karadžić?'

It was the question I had been burning to ask. State? Church? The RS? His family? His bodyguards? Was it the Americans . . . the French? Or was he really just 'by himself'?

My informant gave me a half smile.

'Let us just say that he was protected by friends. By people who believed in him and thought it would simply be wrong if he were transferred to The Hague. That is not to say that those individuals believed in his total innocence. In fact, some believed he did have some serious questions to answer. But they also believed that The Hague was not the right place for him to answer those questions. Elements within the Serbian state certainly knew where he was, especially in the last months. But it all came down to politics in the end. Serbia was, and is, changing. The sands of time were running out for Radovan Karadžić and maybe he felt it too.'

'So how was he finally found and arrested? What happened at the end?'

'He knew he was under surveillance. But he also knew there was nothing he could do about it. The government changed. People in important positions left their jobs and new people came in. I cannot give the precise sequence of events because, honestly, I do not know. It was not a single mistake, a single intercepted phone call, someone suddenly recognising him in the street. What happened was that critical mass had been reached. It was finally considered beneficial for the arrest to be made.

'He had been under surveillance for some time. He was followed on to the number seventy-three bus. It was not clear what his [final] destination was. We do not think he was going far, but they evidently thought it was better to be safe than sorry. At the pre-arranged moment, the bus was pulled over. He was taken off without a struggle. He was interrogated by the Serbian intelligence service, his belongings were searched and examined. A few days later his bag was taken back to the scene of the arrest and dumped. You must understand, there were great sensitivities involved. They obviously thought they had to be careful. The driver of the bus was told to go and take a holiday in Bosnia. They wanted it all to be neat and tidy.'

He began to zip up his coat and prepare to leave.

'I hope some of this has been useful,' he said, offering me his hand.

'Yes, thank you. It has been very, very interesting.' I ignored his hand. 'But I still need to know something . . .' He had already started walking away. I hastened after him, our footsteps echoing on the stone floor. I could hear our shadow closing in fast behind me.

It was a bright morning outside. The snow had largely disappeared and the sun was already rising between the houses of the village. The sky was blue with just the odd cloud. The dew on the grass sparkled in the sun's rays. I caught up with him and grabbed his arm. I was very aware of the third man standing close behind me.

'Tell me,' I said, 'why should I believe anything you have said? I don't know who you are . . . your name . . . nothing.'

He frowned.

'Test me. Ask me something that has not been in the public

206

domain, in a newspaper or on TV. Ask me something you know but no one else does.'

I thought suddenly of the sketch that Dudurović had drawn in my notebook: the floorplan of the flat in Yuri Gagarin Street.

'Describe the flat. Can you describe the place where he lived?'

'You walk in. The bathroom is on the right, the kitchen on the left. When you walk through the hallway, it opens out into the living room. That's where his desk was. There were a lot of books. The one and only bedroom was to the right. Satisfied?'

The speed and confidence with which he described the plan of the flat was convincing.

'Do you know anything about a man called Dudurović?'

'Karadžić met him at the Innovation Fair in Belgrade. They became good friends.'

'Do you know of an event involving Karadžić in Saint Mark's Church, in the centre of Belgrade?'

For a moment he seemed thrown. But not for long.

'Of course. He was lighting a candle in the church and had put his bag down. I think it had his *visaks* and his mobile phones in. When he turned round after lighting the candle, The bag had gone. Very suspicious.' He half smiled.

'Can I get in touch with you if I need to follow up on any of this?' I asked.

'Maybe. I will be in touch with you.' We finally shook hands and he left the churchyard, his companion at his heels.

I met my informant for the last time a few weeks later. I wanted to go over his story once more. Everything added up. But there was one other question I wanted to ask. Did he know if Karadžić had attended his mother's funeral? The answer was no, he had watched it afterwards on video.

I never found out who my 'Deep Throat' was, or who he worked for, if anyone. But I was satisfied he had told me the truth. And I could not forget that what he told me chimed in with what I had been told by Del Ponte and the spy in the Sarajevo restaurant – that they believed Karadžić was hiding in Belgrade. They had been right all along.

I had spent most of the previous six years on the trail of Europe's most wanted man. I had met many people, been to many places. I had been given false information and false leads. I had encountered bigotry and hatred; met people who had suffered more than I could imagine.

I had also had the good fortune to view this story from many angles. From the cosseted offices of the international community in Bosnia, I had observed how those hunting Radovan Karadžić did not speak with one voice; how, in fact, they did not act in unison or with the same goals. From the corridors of power in Belgrade I had witnessed the internal political strife as the leadership fought off threats from the extremists while at the same time trying to present a new and positive image to the world. From the homes of the dispossessed and powerless I had witnessed the very real consequences of war and the desire for that elusive thing called justice.

I had hoped, one way or another, to find Radovan Karadžić and ideally to interview him. But it was not to be. Nevertheless, after investing so much of my time and energy, I had to complete the circle. I decided to go to The Hague and actually see him for myself.

15

Through the Looking Glass

'Radovan Karadžić is now in the custody of the International Criminal Tribunal for the former Yugoslavia. After 13 years at large, he arrived in the Netherlands early this morning. The arrest is immensely important for the victims who had to wait far too long for this day. It is also important for international justice because it clearly demonstrates that there is no alternative to the arrest of war criminals and that there can be no safe haven for fugitives.' – Serge Brammertz, Chief Prosecutor, The Hague, 30 July 2008

Radovan Karadžić walked into the room no more than three metres away from where I was sitting. We were separated by a glass wall. I willed him to look in my direction, but he did not. I had imagined a moment like this occurring in a secluded room in a mountain-top monastery in Montenegro, or a wooden hut in a clearing in a snow-covered forest in the Bosnian wilderness, even in a smoky, rundown bar in the back-streets of the Serbian capital. Instead it would be here, in this sterile courtroom in the Netherlands.

Karadžić had already appeared in court on a couple of occasions, his appearances all short and focused on procedural details. It would be several months before his trial would actually start. I wanted to observe him for as long as possible and to hear more of the substance of the case. My opportunity had now arisen. His close friend and former colleague, Momčilo

Krajišnik, had called on his old political master to be a defence witness in his case.

Krajišnik and Karadžić went back a long way. In the mid-1980s they had served jail time together after they both became embroiled in a controversial construction scheme. At the outbreak of war Krajišnik had been Speaker of the Bosnian Parliament and was known to have good relations with the Muslim President, Alija Izetbegović. As war threatened Sarajevo, the two men even held a secret meeting in the city in order to try to avert disaster. The meeting failed and war erupted.

Krajišnik became Speaker of the Bosnian Serb Parliament which set itself up in Pale. There he had been very close to Karadžić and often attended Bosnian Serb Presidency meetings. It is a matter of dispute whether he was ever actually a member of the Presidency during the war. Afterwards, he served as the Serb representative on the three-member Bosnian Presidency, along with a Croat and a Muslim, doing everything he could to protect the legacy of his former patron who by that time had gone into hiding.

Krajišnik was unaware that there was a sealed indictment against him from The Hague. Sealed (or rather, secret) indictments were often used by the Tribunal so that those being targeted would not be forewarned that an arrest operation might be launched against them. In April 2000 he was arrested by French NATO troops in Pale and transferred to The Hague. After a two-and-half-year-long trial in 2006, he was found guilty of war crimes and sentenced to 27 years in jail. He had appealed against this sentence and, when Radovan Karadžić was arrested, saw the opportunity to call his old friend and ally as a witness for the defence. The court gave Karadžić permission to appear.

On arriving in The Hague the previous day, I had gone straight to the prison where Karadžić and other defendants were being held. It was situated in an upmarket residential district. The taxi brought me to a long, tree-lined avenue. At first I thought the driver had dropped me off in the wrong place. Then, looking around, I noticed the upper storey of a large building that had been concealed by some houses standing in front of it. I could just make out bars at the windows. I found the entrance and walked up to the reinforced glass window of the reception desk.

The United Nations Detention Centre at Scheveningen, on the outskirts of the city, had been established in 1995. It was not a long-term prison for those found guilty of crimes in the former Yugoslavia but rather a remand centre for those either awaiting or in the process of their trial. Serbs, Croats, Muslims and Albanians (from the Kosovo conflict) were all held there; the facilities were mixed and not divided by ethnic group or nationality.

This had led to all sorts of speculation about how the various individuals detained there were getting on with each other. Former enemies were now sharing the same showers, cooking utensils and Scrabble boards. Were there arguments over who would play whom at table soccer or whose turn it was to use the coffee percolator?

In Sarajevo there was a rumour going round that the Serb rabble-rouser Vojislav Šešelj, and the Muslim leader Naser Orić, who had defended Srebrenica against the Serbs, had met each other in the detention unit's gym. Apparently they had got on so well that they ended up helping each other as they had done sit-ups. Was that true or just another stranger than life Balkan myth?

There was certainly nothing fantastical about the calibre of these detention facilities for prisoners accused of some of the most horrific crimes to have occurred in Europe for a generation. The detention block not only had state-of-the-art security systems, its corridors, facilities, cells and communal areas were all constructed to the highest standard. Each prisoner had a fifteen-square-metre en-suite cell, equipped with computer, bed, shelves, hand basin and toilet. Guards monitored the inmates through reinforced glass panels in the doors. Some of the cells also had CCTV. The communal facilities included a socialising area with board games, satellite TV and a kitchen where inmates could cook their own food. Newspapers from the former Yugoslavia and a small library were provided. There were classrooms where prisoners could study: English, computer and art classes were the most popular. There were also up-to-date sports facilities: a well-equipped gym and sports hall where they could play football, volleyball and squash. Punch bags were available. There were also well-equipped medical facilities.

Serbs generally had a pathological hatred of The Hague Tribunal, mainly because, over the years, the vast majority of defendants there had been Serbs. The view was that the court was anti-Serb and was only administering 'victor's justice', i.e. the will of the United States and its allies who had bombed the Serbs into ending the Bosnian War and bombed them again to stop the onslaught against Albanians in Kosovo in 1999. The Serbs felt that responsibility for the wars of the 1990s should be attributed more equally; that more Muslims, Croats and Albanians should have been on trial.

Over time, people of all nationalities were indeed convicted by the Tribunal, confirming that war crimes were committed by all sides. But what most Serbs still failed to accept was that, quite simply, more war crimes had been committed by their side. They preferred to cling to a popular conspiracy theory in the Balkans that the wars were caused by some grand coalition of Western politicians, big American business and radical Islam, and the Serbs made them their scapegoats.

On the morning of Karadžić's appearance as a witness, I grabbed the first taxi from the central railway station and asked the driver to take me to the UN War Crimes Court. It was 8.30. I knew he was due to appear in court at 9 a.m. Ten minutes later the taxi pulled up outside an anonymous grey office building in the centre of the city. The driver turned round expectantly.

'Er . . . this isn't it,' I said. The driver looked confused. 'Listen, I need to go to the UN War Crimes Court . . . you know, the one for the former Yugoslavia where Carla Del Ponte was the prosecutor. The one that's on TV all the time.' The driver's face brightened. We set off again.

After another ten minutes, having left the centre of the city, we arrived at a grand old building set in its own grounds and topped with a very high tower. This was where the United Nations International Court of Justice was based, an entirely different body from the Tribunal I sought. I glanced at my watch. It was 8.50. I was going to be late. I emphasised in the strongest possible terms to the driver that he was wrong again and that now I was going to be late for a very important appointment. This seemed to focus his mind and we shot off. Five minutes later, we pulled up outside the International Criminal Tribunal for the Former Yugoslavia.

I did not leave the taxi driver a big tip. After rushing to the guardhouse outside the main building and showing my passport, I walked through the metal detectors and deposited my mobile phone in a special locker. In order to get to Courtroom 1, where the appeal hearing was due to take place, I had to pass through another metal detector and was then directed up a sweeping staircase to the left. I took the stairs two at a time. At the top, a blue-uniformed guard stopped me and asked for the pass that I had been given in the guardhouse. I had been expecting a door to lead into the courtroom. Instead, the guard pointed to some screens behind him. I grabbed a set of headphones from a table, in case I needed an interpreter, then went through the screens.

Behind a huge glass wall was Courtroom 1. I was evidently in the public gallery and press area. I walked to the front row of chairs and sat down. The courtroom was already full of judges, lawyers and court officials and I could see on the left-hand side the defendant's box with Momčilo Krajišnik installed in it. Guards were sitting to either side of him.

Lawyers, clerks, judges, the accused, were all crammed together in this crucible of justice. God knows who designed the interior. Yellow walls clashed with the grey carpet, and the blue and light brown curtains hanging behind and near the bench where the three judges were sitting. In the corners were cameras and speakers, and, at either end of the rectangular room, slightly elevated glass booths where the interpreters were sitting. Suddenly all eyes turned in the direction of the door to my left. With a confident step, Radovan Karadžić strode in. It was 9.08 a.m.

He was wearing a dark suit, red tie and light pink shirt. He walked bolt upright with his head held high as if defying the court. His jacket looked slightly too big, cuffs falling over his wrists. He sat down in the witness's seat just in front me; fumbled with his headphones for a translation before placing them over his ears. Although his English was very good, he preferred to use his own language in court. His Dragan Dabić beard and grey-white pony-tail had disappeared. Now his hair was combed back into the familiar bouffant style. He had become quite jowly, not surprising for someone in their early-sixties. One hand disappeared into a pocket and he brought out some black-framed reading glasses. When he put them on, he assumed an almost intellectual air.

The lawyer acting for him was introduced to the court. He was there to make sure any answers Karadžić gave in defence of Krajišnik could not, in turn, be used against him when his own trial began. For the next hour, the Prosecution tried hard to question the witness but, more often than not, the former President's lawyer would jump up and object, accusing them of fishing for information.

Radovan Karadžić gave the impression that he revelled in all the attention. At times he was asked to read documents in English and it was clear he had not lost any of his fluency in the language over the years. At other times he would become animated and gesticulate with his right hand. His voice was soft with just the hint of a lisp. He seemed almost apologetic when he had to disagree with whatever the Prosecution was suggesting to him. It was a strong performance.

Eventually the judges called for a 20-minute break while the tapes of proceedings were changed and, presumably, to give the interpreters a rest. Karadžić's shoulders relaxed. I stood up and walked towards the glass partition. At the same time Karadžić rose from his chair and his lawyer approached him. Both of them were smiling as they shook hands. They obviously felt it had been a successful opening and were probably justified in this. The Prosecution had failed to land a significant punch on either Krajišnik or his witness. I stared at Karadžić. So this was the great hero, leader, President, poet, doctor. This was the war criminal, evil mastermind, the man who had turned a blind eye to murder and rape, the man ultimately to blame for the disaster that engulfed Bosnia.

I decided to take a break myself, and had one sip of a strong, cold cappuccino from a machine in the reception area as I reflected on the fact that, after all this time, I had finally laid eyes on Karadžić in the flesh. To be honest, it had been something of an anti-climax. My heart had pumped faster when he stepped into the courtroom and I had been utterly transfixed by my first glimpse of him, examining every detail of his attire, absorbed in his every move and gesture. But nothing I had seen had really come as a surprise. It was as though I had already known him for years.

I left the rest area to stretch my legs and stopped outside something called the UN ICTY Gift Shop. It looked like it had not been cleaned for years. There were a few dusty T-shirts, some rucksacks and a row of tea cups. I looked at the shop's contents, wondering who would actually buy these items. Would the families of the accused or witnesses to a massacre really want to remember the day they visited The Hague Tribunal by buying a tatty little rucksack?

I walked to the far end of the hall where any further advance was prevented by another glass wall and some revolving doors controlled by electronic passes. Beyond were the offices of the judges and clerks. A few feet away hung a huge sign declaring: 'UN ICTY – bringing war criminals to justice . . . and justice to victims'.

Was that what the victims really thought? Had The Hague brought them justice?

At the reception desk I asked if I could speak to a court official about the possibility of interviewing the former Bosnian Serb President. I was told, 'Generally there is a rule that journalists cannot do interviews with those being held.

Only lawyers and family and possibly close friends can see defendants.'

It was time to return to the courtroom. As I resumed my seat, a class of laughing, chattering high school students started filing into the public gallery. At the same moment, Karadžić returned. I expected at least some hush from the children but there was barely a break in the hubbub. Did they even know who this person was or were the dark days of the Bosnian War just another tedious subject in school to them?

The session resumed. Karadžić's lawyer continued to raise technical objections. A couple of interesting points did emerge, though. On describing the setting up of his SDS Party, Karadžić said that its founders were a large group of Serb dissidents from Communist days who:

> ... refused to establish a political party on an ethnic basis. However, the SDA [political party] had already been established as the party of the Muslim people, and the HDZ [mainly Croat political party] spilled over from Croatia ... it became clear that the Serb people had to have a party of their own or to vote for the Communists.

At another point Karadžić insisted he had never really wanted to be leader:

> I never wanted to be the President of the Republic but had to accept it in the end ... I was always reticent but I thought that it was difficult for one man to make those decisions, so I always relied on more people. However, here it is quite clear and it is stressed that the Presidency was us three, the three of us [referring to Plavšić and Koljević, the other members of the Presidency at that time].

When the hearing was over, I wandered slowly back down the winding staircase. Spotting Karadžić's lawyer at the bottom, I walked straight up to him and introduced myself. I asked him if there would be any possibility of interviewing his client. He said that personally he was in favour and he was certain that his client would be delighted. He had already put in a formal request for Karadžić to be allowed to do interviews, but he was not optimistic.

He indicated that when their own trial began they were very much pursuing the line that there had been a deal with Richard Holbrooke and that this was likely to be a key argument in their defence.

I walked down to the sea front. The sun was out and clouds were racing in over the North Sea. I watched the white surf breaking on the sand. To my right was a long pier with a restaurant at the end. I could see an oil tanker in the distance, moving almost imperceptibly over the horizon. A young couple strolled along the beach, laughing and smiling, their dog racing ahead. A bright red balloon suddenly bobbed out from under the pier and surged into the air.

My quest for Radovan Karadžić was over. I turned away from the beach and ambled along the promenade. Up ahead I could see some television cameras. They were filming an episode of a Dutch comedy series. I stood and watched the actors rehearse their lines. The director, sitting a few feet away outside one of the fast food bars, intent on his TV monitor, called for 'Action!' A baby started crying in a pram nearby and the mother glanced towards me, a little embarrassed, perhaps thinking I was part of the film crew.

Less than three hours away by plane were Belgrade and Sarajevo and Pale and Petnica and Banja Luka and Srebrenica and New Belgrade. And there were the peacekeepers and the spies and the generals and the priests and the politicians and the war crimes fugitives and the widows. And the hurt and the pain and the sadness and the anger and the frustration and the fear and the desire to move on. In a sense, I felt I had finally completed the circle. Since those initial days after landing in Bosnia six years earlier, I had received quite an education. I had chased a shadow around the former Yugoslavia; witnessed the international community, in all its guises, swagger and stumble its way through another post-war environment; met the peoples and explored the countries of a fascinating part of Europe.

I thought about the valley I had once visited. The one with the rock at its entrance and the ancient inscription, warning people not to defile its slopes and river. Would all those who had nevertheless defiled Bosnia one day face their own day of judgement?

With the capture of Radovan Karadžić, the cloud that I had sensed hanging over the country in those early days was finally dispersing. The pain and the hurt would remain – for so many people of all nationalities. The people who had perished would never come back. Souls that had been broken could not be mended. Many people had played a role in the break-up of the country but some had played a bigger role than others. It was important that justice should catch up with them, for the sake of future generations and to prove that there was no ultimate escape. My journey had ended in a courtroom in the Netherlands, hundreds of miles away from the place it had begun.

Their scene completed, the actors drifted off to a nearby restaurant and the TV crew started rolling up cables and dismantling equipment. I turned and walked away down the promenade.

Index